THE
LAKE'S
APPRENTICE

THE
LAKE'S
APPRENTICE

ANNAMARIA
WELDON

U W
A P
UWA PUBLISHING

First published in 2014
by UWA Publishing
Crawley, Western Australia 6009
www.uwap.uwa.edu.au

UWAP is an imprint of UWA Publishing
a division of The University of Western Australia

THE UNIVERSITY OF
WESTERN AUSTRALIA

National Library of Australia Cataloguing-in-Publication entry
       Title: The lake's apprentice / Annamaria Weldon
       ISBN: 9781742585574 (paperback)
       Dewey Number: A823.4

Motif of flying birds by Carolyn Marks
Design and typeset in Bembo and Avenir by Anna Maley-Fadgyas
Printed by 1010

THE CHARLES AND JOY STAPLES SOUTH WEST REGION
publications fund was established in 1984 on the basis of a
generous donation to The University of Western Australia
by Charles and Joy Staples.

The purpose of the Fund was to make the results of research on the South
West region of Western Australia widely available. The aim was to assist
the people of the South West region, and those in government and private
organisations concerned with South West projects, to appreciate the needs
and possibilities of the region in the widest possible historical perspective.

The Fund is administered by a committee whose aims are to make possible
the publication (either by full or part funding), by UWA Publishing, of
research in any discipline relevant to the South West region.

An act of pilgrimage in writing. NICOLAS ROTHWELL

CONTENTS

THE PRACTICE OF BELONGING

'There is a practice of belonging and it starts with forgetfulness of self.' MARK TREDINNICK, *The Blue Plateau*

I

Perhaps love is a country discovered
by chance, that you and I tried too hard
to find. Instead, the land we travelled through
last gave me its South West lyric, voiced

my best lines: Nullaki Peninsula
folded like a hinge between twin skies. Slopes
of weathered granite *marooned in low cloud.*

Those headlands *darker than lampblack,* at rest
on a parchment sea. *The inkstone forest*
always in sight, *hunkered as memory.*

Winter sun *streaming chinks in the karri*
tracks *that followed light North to the future.*
At Green's Pool, *water's way of belonging* –
the self-forgetfulness of waves on sand.

2

We've lingered. Because this is wine country.
Slow parting tastes sweet as a vine's late grapes.
I'd call it grace, but you already know
this is a place of parables. Outside

your window, a kookaburra's flying
the unseen, remembered skyway between
branches, gliding fast across the clearing

in those low, wide parabolas birds hitch
to burl and bark. But the sleeping boobook
becomes a wood carving, enters the tree
and leaves without a wing-beat, dissolving

in a shadow-screen. Look, you say to me
at his way of belonging – this gradual
arrival that begins with letting go.

PART I

Essays
Photos
Nature notes

NATURE NOTES
meeting the river

This is ecology of residence. The Latin root of residence means staying in one place a long time.[1]

My main preoccupation for the past five years has been the creation story of Yalgorup – a coastal national park in the Peel–Harvey catchment area of Mandurah and Pinjarra – and how its wetlands embody this tradition, which is so central to Bindjareb Noongar culture. Like a circle, this story begins and ends with my heartfelt gratitude for the welcome and guidance I have received. It's a story told with respect for Bindjareb elders past and present, love for their knowledge of ancestors, country and language, with yearning for deeper appreciation of those relationships which endure between them, and sustain us all.

It is also the story of my gradual attunement to Yalgorup's wetlands and the Lake Clifton thrombolites at its centre: how I became the lake's apprentice and my estrangement was transformed to endemophilia. Glenn Albrecht created this term, endemophilia, to capture in one word the particular love of the locally and regionally distinctive elements of place for its people.[2] I lost this once-familiar state of heartmind and embodied experience three decades ago on leaving Malta, my natal island. Writing down my own ecology

of residence brought about my second birth, the one I had been waiting for without knowing it, not understanding why I didn't feel quite at home here in Western Australia, yet.

George Walley was, from the beginning, a cultural guide and mentor; the first to recognise and affirm my growing attachment to his country. The deepening conversation with place and people which he mediated became the ground I traversed on my way home to Yalgorup. George's teaching style and his attitude to embodied knowledge are very subtle, a constant reminder of the difference between Indigenous ways of knowing nature and the western way of sourcing information through research and interviews. I had known the former, being an islander by birth, and then learnt to forget it during years of training and working as a journalist. So at my first meeting with George, I plied him with direct questions. What should I look out for and write about at the wetlands? Was it long-necked turtles? Tuarts? Black cockatoos? What else was significant?

Before this siege of words began, I had been showing George my early photos of the Yalgorup lakes. We'd been concurring about the landscape, especially the exquisite quality of its light viewed from the viewing platform at Lake Clifton, where it reveals every feature and, paradoxically, makes

a unity of sky and water, sun and earth, such as I saw in the snowscapes of my childhood. And yet the light is not the same everywhere: on land, it appears in striations, progressing from the high canopies of tuart down through peppermint to the understory vegetation, then the windswept reeds, and finally the samphire and rockpools of the bleached, shoreline thrombolite reef. On the lakebed, ribbons of light become golden nets, and its dazzle on the surface a never-ending discourse with the wind. Each silver or golden strand of light is quite distinct on land, where it shimmers through the different degrees of albedo – the luminosity reflected by each surface and a word I would come to know well at the wetlands. Months later, at the lake, I observed George as he watched the light shifting subtly through these horizontal lines, like a finely nuanced language he could read or hear.

As well as talking about this light, George alluded to a significant aspect of the Bindjareb

Noongar creation story, the Woggaal's eggs, which are known to non-Aboriginal people as the Lake Clifton thrombolites, and he seemed delighted at my association of this traditional story, so central to his tradition, with contemporary scientific theory which deems microbialites responsible for raising Earth's early atmospheric oxygen levels through their photosynthetic processes, thus enabling other life forms to exist. It was all going well, I thought, childishly pleased that George liked my pictures so much. Thrombolites are as photogenic as they are fascinating; I had captured them through the seasons, inundated in winter and exposed in summer, documenting seasonal shifts

and surrounding water–light effects. Whatever I've
learned about taking photos was gleaned informally
from my father. Obsessed by celluloid, he owned a
number of still and movie cameras, had a keen eye
for composition, and was patient and perceptive about
details. Perhaps it is thanks to his lifelong passion that
several of my images have been published, and many
capture the wetlands' dream-like quality. George said
that he particularly liked this aspect, and kept right on
looking at them when I (concerned at the limited time
we had for George is very busy) started questioning
him and shifted to accelerated interviewing mode. We
were sitting in the courtyard at Fremantle Arts Centre,
and while we were looking at the photos in silence, a
willy wagtail landed on the table between us, chirping
and dancing. But then it flew away, and I noticed
(without registering why) that George was leaning
further and further back in his chair. At last, becoming
aware of his stillness and my own urgency, I stopped

talking. Then George smiled at me and, gesturing at my pictures, simply said, 'No need to ask. There are portals everywhere at Yalgorup, and you've found them already. Just be there with an open heart'.

I did as he suggested. Many seasons passed. One day I asked George if it would be appropriate for me to visit the Murray River site of the historic Pinjarra Massacre of 1834. Located some kilometres inland from Lake Clifton and the national park, the site is nonetheless within the Bindjareb cultural region and part of the Peel–Harvey catchment area, connected traditionally and hydrographically to the coastal wetland. Beginning to sense that my immersion in the area was incomplete, I felt the need to know more about this event and explore its terrain.

'Go before the anniversary', George advised, and started to draw directions. When the arrows of his map began to run off the Dome Cafe's paper napkin, he looked up and said, 'I'll take you there myself'. And that's how, a few days before 28 October, in the mild sunlight of that season which Noongar people call Kambarang, I came to be standing high on a bank above the Murray, awkwardly clutching some red roses and some white roses from my garden. I had known we were going to a significant memorial place and was unsure what to take. So before making any gestures of respect, I listened to George relate the story and speak aloud in his own language. His acknowledgment to ancestral country and this river, the very river bend where he was born fifty years earlier, resonated in the morning air. It was incantatory yet conversational, reverent as a prayer and personal as a greeting. I noticed how all the black-faced sheep grazing on the opposite bank lifted their heads and stood absolutely still, in a single line, watching him.

Kindly, and patient as always, George translated for me, later writing down phrases and spelling out each word. But mostly, we just sat, and watched, and listened to the wind, to the birds and river. My memory of that morning is of unhurried time, of being present without the need for conversation.

Mid-morning he mentioned another significant spot further along that we should visit. It was a kilometre south-west, and here we were able to walk through dense riparian vegetation right down to where the river lapped a shallow cove. The ground was silty, and there were small red-stained patches of sand, some kind of mineral deposit, I supposed. George leaned over the water and washed his hands and face, then sat down. So I did the same. Time and the river flowed on. Eventually he said that he was going to take off his

boots and wade in. 'Should I do that?' 'If you'd like to. We won't go in far', he reassured me.

The water was clear, tannin-stained to dark amber, cool around my ankles. River sand, soft and fine, seeped between my toes. The flowing water slowly carried past tiny white stamen, like seams of long tacking stitched to its skin. These had drifted down from the flowering flooded gums which line the Murray's banks. Water insects dipped, dappling the surface with circles or skimming along it with trailing wakes. Great gnarled roots and the aged branches of fallen trees reared up from their reflections, semi-sunken limbs gesturing from the shallows.

Because I am an outsider to Noongar culture, what George did next surprised me. Even though I've had strong emotional and even physical responses to many places through my life, the Catholic tradition in which I was raised certainly didn't encourage a personal, spiritual relationship to the land, let alone its outward expression. But George addressed the river once more, along with the surrounding country, its elements, creatures and plants in a firm voice, and this time it was to tell them about me. He said I was a storyteller, a poet who came in friendship. He told Bilya Maadjit – for that is the river's traditional name – to know, recognise and welcome me. He asked that knowledge of this place and its story be with me whenever I wrote of it, wherever I may be. George spoke in Bindjareb, translating for my benefit every now and then. And when he had finished, he suggested I speak to the river, to country, aloud, as he had done. 'Speak simply and from your heart, and they will know you. For everything in the nature we see around us is totem. It is the living ancestors'.

When our visit was almost complete, we went to the small stone memorial, high on the bank under a grove of trees, by the busy road to Pinjarra. It is an unremarkable place: peaceful and shady enough when the traffic abates. I found it sad and strange that there are no road signs or interpretive boards indicating this is the location of a significant memorial. No names of the deceased are inscribed on the stone, nor is the word 'massacre' sanctioned by the local shire. It seems that the trauma of old wounds is deep, and carried by both sides, though only written officially by one.

After George Walley had cut down and given me a branch of river gum – kooloodoo[3] – to take home, we left. That was when he told me to say, if I told this story, that the massacre site was 'a very strong place' and therefore being taken through the proper customs was important for my own protection. And I ought to point out, he added, that there is a different way – which he could not tell me about – of introducing a male visitor to the river. 'I just love this country', I said. And without missing a beat, George replied 'It loves you right back'.

1   Diane Fouts, 'At The Owl in Kane Creek', article in *Ecology of Residency* (2009), an online magazine which features works from the Ecology of Residency class, part of the Environmental Humanities Graduate Program at The University of Utah, viewed 17 July 2013, <http://www.ecologyofresidency.utah.edu/?p=72&cpage=1#comment-9>.

2   Endemophilia: an emplaced and home-based counter-term to traditionally defined nostalgia. The English word, 'endemic', is based on the French word, *endémique* and has the Greek roots, *endēmia* (a dwelling in) and *endēmos* (native in the people) and *philia* (love of). Endemophilia captures in one word the particular love of the locally and regionally distinctive elements of a place for its people. See: G. A. Albrecht, 'Psychoterratic conditions in a scientific and technological world', in P. Kahn and P. Hasbach (eds), *Ecopsychology: Science, Totems, and the Technological Species*, MIT Press, Cambridge, Massachusetts, 2012, pp. 241–64.

3   George's name for *Eucalyptus rudis*, the flooded gums which he refers to as 'river gums', which is what I've called them in my poem 'The memory of earth', written after this visit and subsequently published in *Westerly*, vol. 56, no.1, pp. 96–7. Common spellings are *kulurda* and *moitch*.

THRESHOLD COUNTRY

I'm drawn to country between wetlands and sea
sand over limestone, like the shore
where I left my other skin
before I became estuarine
sweetwater on brine.[1]

Mandurah is country inscribed with the passage of water, sweet and salt, in drought or inundation, above ground, underground. Its tidal flow, inland from the Western Australian coast through the Dawesville Channel, flushes Peel Inlet and Harvey Estuary where the Serpentine, Murray and Harvey rivers return to the ocean. The Peel–Harvey region is shaped by water's restless cursive, its tidal narrations of exile and arrival. Only at Yalgorup Lakes does water lie pooled and tideless, trapped between dunes, dreaming of the nearby sea it came from long ago.

The city of Mandurah is one of Australia's fastest growing regional centres. Transformed over the past thirty years, some of the fishing-village ambience many remember from modest family holidays is now overshadowed by the high-rise real estate typical of baby boomers' sea-change nirvanas. Famous for ocean and estuary beaches, boating and fishing, Mandurah is being landscaped for tourist complexes and canal homes.

But thirty kilometres south of the city, along the Old Coast Road, once its main link to Bunbury, is another world: Yalgorup National Park, a 13,000 ha coastal strip of limestone and sand dunes with Ramsar-listed wetlands nestled in their folds.[2] Here, salted scrub and stands of mallee give way to swamp paperbarks and peppermints. Remnant tuart forest is stranded between land and sea, and timescales meet at the ecotone of Quindalup and Spearwood dunes. Here, land holds history the way lakes hold reflections on their surface, the way Lake Clifton holds fossils shaped like memories under its skin.

This country immerses you, wraps its stories round you, makes you care about them: the curlew sandpipers which fly here from Siberia; the long-necked turtles who labour to lay their eggs where they will not fall prey to eagles or hawks; the hooded plovers whose chicks may not hatch, crushed in their eggs on shallow sand-scrapes at a lake's shore; the ancient rock-like mounds, more than two thousand years old, still growing at Lake Clifton though they have become remnant fossils in other lakes.

They are called thrombolites, lacustrine fossils formed by an accretion of residue from photosynthetic bacteria at their living edge. Like so much else in the wetlands, the active microorganisms are susceptible to alterations in habitat. Their story stands in counterpoint to the scale and pace of urban life and puts Mandurah's recent, rapid expansion into perspective: the thrombolites are at least two thousand years old and they grow just 0.1–1.0 mm higher each year.[3]

This was not the story I planned to write. I was on my way to the South West's karri and granite country when I came across Yalgorup. And though it felt like love at first sight, I didn't trust my feelings: I was wary of getting involved with another place between land and sea, one which evoked too many features of the windswept, salt-encrusted limestone island I had left behind two decades earlier. The intervening years were spent trying to free my roots from their Mediterranean bedrock, becoming 'Australian'. But a hidden lake and the precarious living rocks at its heart drew me in. Getting to know them and telling the story has, in unexpected ways, finally taken me across that threshold, the one we don't know is there until the day we feel at home in a place.

'*Our* stories about who we are all begin somewhere else.'[4] Yalgorup country, too, won't forget where it came from: its land and water are heavy with the memory of sea. Ten lakes, some brackish and some saline, resulted from alternating ocean levels during this last interglacial period. As they rose and fell, water flowed inland and back. Gradually, as the coastal profile changed, spreading dunes sealed the outlets and trapped residual water. Aerial views of Yalgorup today show these lakes as a brilliant blue chain running north to south in three long strands, parallel to the coast. But at ground level, even bathed in the famous Western Australian light, Yalgorup's bushland, sand hills and lakes are enigmatic and unfathomable.

It's a place of shorelines and sheltered habitats. Each ecotone evokes a litany of names for edge, those margins and thresholds where life must adapt to survive and grow. This is what the thrombolites have done at Lake Clifton. They look like low circular columns broken off at the base, edges worn smooth and round by water and wind. Those in deepest water are conical and can reach over a metre in height, with girths to match. When exposed by falling lake levels due to summer evaporation, their surface becomes brittle as dry sponge. Each one is distinct, with cracks and whorls on its domed surface as individual as signs of age on a tree, or a human face.

These remarkable rocks are so friable that before the lake's viewing platform was built, many were crushed by careless visitors. Complex communities of microscopic organisms are housed within their stony structures: they live like orders of anchorites, dependent on symbiotic relationships with each other and the walls growing around them. The minute cyanobacteria are vulnerable to environmental shifts. Their photosynthetic process relies on freshwater springs which bubble up under them as they grow in the benthic mud and vital clear water.

In a fossil removed for geological research, I saw the tiny canal which spring water had left in the core of a thrombolite after thousands of years.[5] The springs on Lake Clifton's eastern shore are rich in calcium carbonate, from which the precipitate, cemented by mucus-like secretions, is derived. Unlike coral, which actively grows its own exoskeleton, thrombolite mounds, also known as microbialites, are formed by a passive process, including chemical reaction with the brackish water around them. Each alteration to groundwater flow, nutrient concentrations, the lake's salinity or its rainfall-dependent winter inundation challenges their survival.

The thrombolites have lived here for thousands of years due to rare and successful adaptation: in summer they are almost totally exposed and in winter, when run-off and rain raise the water level, they are fully submerged. Clifton's lake-bound microbialite reef is the largest in the southern hemisphere, extending over four square kilometres. Now its viability is threatened by encroaching development.

Often confused with stromatolites, thrombolites have 'clotted' internal structures, whereas stromatolites are layered. While these internal architectures are significant to geologists and scientists, it was the striking pattern they made along the shoreline which caught my attention. Summer was ending and the waterline had receded, exposing the reef. As far as I could see, for kilometres north and south along the edge of the blue lake, thousands of bone-white stones were arrayed like dots. I had never seen a landscape like it. My first impression was of a traditional Aboriginal dot painting and its encoded message. It was as though the thrombolites were forming sentences, strung from words of a lost dialect. I tried to listen, wanting to understand, but heard only the rhythmic lap of water against the pylons, wind soughing in the sedges.

Residues of that first encounter have stayed with me. Studying the thrombolites has not dispelled a sense of their eloquent mystery. Even now, when the fossils closest to the viewing platform jetty have become so familiar that I recognise each one's distinct markings, the memory lingers, like a half-lost language forgotten for lifetimes. It is not forgotten by the Bindjareb Noongar, this land's first people. They know that thrombolites, which they call Woggaal Noorook, are eggs laid at Yalgorup in the Dreamtime by the female creation serpent as she travelled south from the Swan River. George,[6] who has helped me to learn his local landscape like a second language, told me this creation story.

Despite a very active Indigenous cultural presence in Mandurah, casual visitors do not find Yalgorup's heart so accessible. The park is not dramatic in quite the manner hurried tourists expect: its wildlife is recondite, seasonal or nocturnal; the low-profile terrain, impenetrable bush and scrub-covered dunes are (in my experience at least) more likely to reveal their intricacies to those who return often, inclined to slip inside the quiet.

With just a few areas around the national park available for day-use or camping, it's not overtly recreational, unless you are drawn to isolated tracks and meditative stretches of water. You have to climb up a ridge or steep park look-out to catch other views. Between dunes, you can see only as far as the nearest row of sandhills; in dense bush, only the trees and grasses of a single thicket; through a lakeside track's fringing trees, pieces of jade water – an unmade jigsaw puzzle.

But to me the lakes are a book of hours in a library of dunes, with aquifers for archives. One story floats over another. These wetlands are a palimpsest of water writing, some layers visible, others unseen. No two lakes at Yalgorup share the same chemistry; each has its own distinct setting, flora and fauna. Elongated Lake Preston is closest to the coast. Behind the next ridge, lakes are grouped like little islands of an archipelago. Travelling north to south, they are Swan Pond, Duck Pond, Boundary Lake, Lake Pollard, Martins Tank

Lake, Lake Yalgorup, Lake Hayward and Newnham Lake. Nearest to the Old Coast Road is Lake Clifton, over twenty kilometres long. Its lakebed, inscribed with histories, lies silent and unread. The thrombolites are not the only memories it keeps under its surface; there is knowledge of early Bindjareb fishing traditions; the wounds of invasion, of exploration and massacre; long scars left by the marl miners, who took its sand and mud to seal the roads of Perth; splinters of a mast, the remnants of a tragic afternoon in 1886 when the Herron children's sailing boat capsized, its mast stuck fast in benthic mud and only two of the four siblings on board eventually made it back to shore.[7]

Every Australian landscape that matters has its lost children, the voices of myth and story whisper. But I suspect Yalgorup has foundlings, too. I spend so much time there just listening and watching, like a child being told stories. What is it that intrigued me from the beginning? Perhaps I've never grown out of my childhood attraction to strangeness: when I first saw this country, despite all that water it seemed calcified, cryptic and sclerophyllous. And yet, bore a striking resemblance to that other place where I once belonged – but left. The broken bond between islander and island was a deeply private pain, as embodied memories so often are. When I discovered Yalgorup, by which I mean when I began to know and relate to it as a special place, that old wound ached like a badly set bone does before rain. Perhaps this was also an augury? I dimly sensed that the terrain had something to tell me, something I needed to learn, about losing a country and recovering a sense of place.

But there was more. As though wholeness regained was significant not only as a personal experience, but as a universal one. I felt this landscape knew I was there.

To geographer Edward Relph, the human sense of place is a synaesthetic faculty which combines sight, hearing, smell, movement, touch, imagination, purpose and anticipation.[8] A complex sense evolved, perhaps, to compensate for our anatomical deficiencies in perception: we have no compound eyes nor the ability to see the ultraviolet spectrum; are unable to taste mammals on the wind, the way a reptile does, with its tongue, or store solar energy through our skin cells as invertebrates do. We have a limited hearing range. We miss the scent of wind-shifts. We are not carried aloft on thermals for a better view. While the creatures around us have nuanced ways of seeing, of being seen by each other, and of knowing the surrounding terrain, we must use our imaginations, our capacity for pattern-finding, for making associations and deriving meaning. We navigate by science but also by story. And it seems to me

24

that at their most authentic, these culturally informed mappings are a deeper wayfinding: they are our way of singing back country, on the inside as well as the outside, until even such distinctions dissolve.

As I began to spend more and more time at Yalgorup, its images and relationships surfaced in the poetry I was writing, shaped its rhythms and layered the textures. In my poems, these were also my images and relationships, the way events and characters of waking life are absorbed into our dreams without losing their haecceity. Rather than imagining country, I was being re-imagined through its lens.

Perhaps the first time I realised this was late in spring, the time between October and November known as Kambarang in the Noongar calendar, while walking with naturalist Laurie Smith,[9] another generous guide, exploring ways to Lake Preston from the seaward side. It was rough ground to cover in the afternoon glare with only occasional ocean gusts to cool us. I began to regret tackling unfamiliar terrain on such a hot day. Tired but determined to complete the trek, I deliberately concentrated on my breathing, the feel of loose rocks skittering underfoot and the crunch of dried leaf litter. It's a simple technique to focus the senses, useful for conserving energy and allaying anxiety.

The unsealed access track cut through aged limestone. I was soon acutely conscious of sharp-edged shadows cast by large rocks and ridges with broken shelves and deep sockets. My vision became keener than usual: I noticed a barely trembling acacia branch the moment before a western yellow robin (*Eopsaltria griseogularis*) launched into flight; spun my head to the right and looked down just in time to see the dramatic leap of a large monitor (probably *Varanus tristis*), airborne at full stretch with its reptilian limbs wide, reaching for a fallen log where it could become invisible as bark, only a tail flick betraying its position as it slid to the shelter of tree roots.

Then something happened for which I barely have words. As though my feet and the ground were joined, the skeletal structure and deep seams of earth and rock beneath my soles seemed tangible as my own flesh and the aching joints where cartilage has worn thin. I felt a country of calcium and salt, cloaked in a sand-skin cast from crushed shells blown off the coast; Yalgorup's limestone ribs, hardened in percolating rain; its lakes, blue veins of a body made from bone and tears, shaped by breath and flood.

When we reached the lake, overwhelmed by a sensation of homecoming, I cupped its water in my palm and wet my lips in greeting, and as a sign. It's the way I've taken sweet offerings of prasad[10] or touched the cooling ash of a sacred fire-pit in other places, at other significant moments. The lake clung to my skin like salt residue from a naming ritual.

26

The names for these landscapes are Mandurah, from Mandjar, meeting place; Pinjarra, which means wetlands; Yalgorup, place of swamps. This is a country of dissolving boundaries. The trees and reeds massed along many shorelines lean out and gaze at themselves in looking-glass lakes. Between their beauty and its reflection, between land and water, is a space where stories are timeless and country is alive. The shady tuart woodlands are filled in with soft peppermint under-storeys, lakes fringed by samphire flats, salt-marshes and swamp paperbarks. Wind and glimmer play in shifting shadows and brushstrokes of light. But it's not a picture, or a framed mirror: this is a place of portals, beckoning the patient visitor to slip inside.

In September's cool dawn, a season called Djilba by this country's first people, I lay quietly at the edge of Lake Hayward under a tangle of low branches, while a family of blue fairy-wrens flitted about just overhead, busily calling to each other. In early May (Djeran time) I sat on Lake Clifton's viewing platform at mid-morning, dangling my bare legs over the water, and watched astounded as a black swan flew straight towards me without veering, then passed by so close I heard the wind rush through its wings. Minutes later, tree martins and welcome swallows, gorged after feeding on newly hatched midge larvae, lined the railings surrounding me, as though I were not there at all or just part of the structure. I knew they had been feeding, because the hatching swarms rose first as wisps, then ribbons and eventually formed dense columns which climbed the sky between the lake's fringing trees in dark spirals, looking so like smoke that several visitors ran for their cars, thinking it was the start of a bushfire. But a drone resembling miniature chainsaws told another story, as millions of insects explored the air.

Such disturbances are rare. There are many places in Yalgorup notable for their stillness and silence, though they don't have the special presence of thrombolites. Baudrillard could have been describing the wetlands when he wrote, 'It is this stillness things dream of, it is this stillness we dream of'.[11]

At Martin Tank, for instance, the paperbarks (*Melaleuca rhaphiophylla* and *M.cuticularis*) grow so close to shore I can slide to the ground, lean my back against a tree-trunk's interleaved softness, then stretch my feet and cool them in the shallows. Each old tree's torso is wrapped in moth-wing layers of papery fibre, bark that hangs down in tissued swatches, forming curled patterns as it peels away. As the folds loosen they rustle in the wind like leaves of old prayer books; shadows fall in paint-strokes on the hollows between whorls, shafts of sun highlight curves and scrolls. Some trees have a pale peach or pink flush to their bark; others are salt white, with dramatic charcoal markings, like shading on a sketch. Their branches, outstretched and sinuous, express different moods in changing light. The tree that seems peaceful as a sage, streaming white hair haloed by the midday sun, can become a tortured soul with gesticulating limbs by dusk. Many are clustered in groves, though like the thrombolites, they are individual, gnarled characters I look forward to visiting.

When I go to Yalgorup alone, I never feel lonely. At Lake Preston, where the causeway to Preston Beach divides the waters into the north and south lakes, I've watched a single kangaroo sit at the lake's edge at daybreak, gazing across the water. That morning it was the middle of Makuru, which is late in June; out on the sandbars avocets, banded stilts and shelducks had stopped feeding and were standing perfectly still on their reflections. It was a landscape on the boundary of day and night; everything paused, waiting for a solstice sun to rise and mark the year's still point. And when it did, all energy seemed focused on that radiance. As it rose above the tree canopy, warming air lifted the fleecy, golden mist which covered the lake. Cleared like breath from glass, it left water polished as an ephemeral mirror in which birds and trees hung motionless under their doubles. Then all changed again. A breeze ruffled the reflections, creatures turned back to feeding. And despite this movement, it seemed the lake held its hypnagogic trance between sleep and dream, where, for a moment, the world within this world is glimpsed.

At Lake Clifton, the thrombolites' ancient presence creates this same impression, no matter what time of year or day I visit. As water ripples round the thrombolites, I'm reminded of South Australian poet John Shaw Neilson's line from 'The crane is my neighbour':[12] 'And the waves are as thoughts coming out to the edge of a dream' and, in the same poem, his description of feathers 'blue as the smoke of summer' comes to mind when I see the white-faced heron which haunts a particular stretch of shallows by the boardwalk. A lifelong love of reading has shaped my perceptions. When I found reference to the wayfarer's way of attention, observation, navigation by signs, by memory, by experience in Beverley Farmer's book *The Bone House*,[13] I wondered: by whose memories and by which signs do I navigate this landscape? Where do they meet?

In both the cultural and the scientific narratives of Yalgorup, thrombolites exist at the boundary between the animate and the inanimate. Researchers, continuing the pioneering work of the late Dr Linda Moore, are still inquisitively mapping the various living forms and functions within each microbial community, unravelling and identifying complex relationships which enable organisms to coexist at an estimated density of 3,000 per square metre.[14] Subsurface upwellings of fresh groundwater within the lake and along the eastern foreshore, are colonised by cyanobacteria that stabilise the carbonate sediment that is precipitated about the point of outflow. The most abundant cyanobacteria within the benthic microbial communities are Scytonema.[15] It has been established through the Pilbara fossils that reefs like those at Lake Clifton existed 3.5 billion years ago and were widely distributed in the oceans. It is highly probable that a type of cyanobacteria[16] enabled life to flourish on earth by increasing the atmospheric oxygen to twenty times its original level.[17]

And the Bindjareb creation story, too, remembers the Woggaal eggs in the beginning.[18]

To me, the thrombolites are akin to Diane James' concept of 'rocks of deep time', which names the transition I feel when at Lake Clifton, as I move away from what she calls 'the surface of shallow time'.[19] They draw energy up from the springs and down from the sunlit sky of the west coast, transforming it into life for themselves and oxygen for the planet. Semi-submerged for half the year, they survive on seasonal inundation and a delicate balance of lacustrine chemistry. These amniotic waters may become embalming if nutrient levels continue to rise due to agriculture and urban sprawl. Can we learn in time to tread more lightly here?

I think, as I write, of reflections on the lake: plants and birds lying weightless on its polished surface, like perfect offerings to the light they came from. There's only a handful of places left on earth where thrombolites still live and grow. In their precariousness, they point not only to life's origins but to that darkening edge which all living things must eventually reach. I think of that time at the end of each day, when the black swans fly in low from the south, necks outstretched. They look like long stitches which night gathers to its far shore, that shore running like a seam through the twilight silk of sky and water.

Darkness and light live here in relationships I have yet to understand, but I suspect it has to do with the line we trace whenever we draw a heart. The line which defines what we love is that same edge we feel so sharply when it is relinquished. Is that the reason why so many of us remain indifferent to country for so long and why so few can name even the trees in our own street? In a nation where half of us are migrants or born of a migrant, with many others dispossessed of their land, is connection to country too painful?

Knowing the names of trees or birds is not, however, knowledge, and only sometimes is it the beginning of understanding or affection. As the Indian sage Krishnamurti cautioned his Western followers, naming something is not the same as seeing it. In Roger McDonald's book, *The Tree in Changing Light*, there is a chapter about the painter Tom Carment, who painted trees because he was interested in the emotional content of the light around them, something he said he could no more give a name to than he could give a name to the trees.[20] I have a great deal of empathy with his attitude.

But there's a place for practical knowledge, which, beyond names and a sense of engagement, demands time and a special kind of attention. Especially to know what is no longer there. Walking at Lake Clifton with Galliano Fardin and his wife Nancy, I suspect it also takes love. They share a nuanced relationship to this land, the familiar intimacy of longtime residents.

Galliano is a reclusive artist whose inspiration comes from the landscape; Nancy's a conservationist making a difference in her community. They live on Lake Clifton's eastern shore in a house they built themselves twenty-five years ago. When they first arrived, there were long-necked turtles (*Chelodina oblonga)*, Carnaby's cockatoos (*Calyptorhynchus latirostris*), boobook owls

(*Ninox novaeseelandiae ocellata*). Now, they told me, there are hardly any. The same is true for banded stilts (*Cladorhynchus leucocephalus*), rainbow bee-eaters (*Merops ornatus*), bats (*Chalinolobus gouldii*) and bungarra, (an Aboriginal name commonly used by Western Australians for the monitor lizard *Varanus gouldii*).[21] They rarely see hooded plovers (*Thinornis rubricollis*), tawny frogmouths (*Podargus strigoides*), western yellow robins (*Eopsaltria griseogularis*) or brown falcons (*Falco berigora*) on their land. New species are moving in, though not all of them are welcome.

The Fardins have planted thousands of trees, re-foresting cleared paddocks, yet only a few hundred seedlings have survived to maturity. They are doing this because the park's tuarts are dying. In some areas of the original tuart forest, here on the Swan Coastal Plain, which is the only part of the world where tuarts occur naturally, they believe the mortality rate is fifty per cent. 'There has been total death of 80 per cent of the mature Tuart trees (*Eucalyptus gomphocephala*) in the area most affected within Yalgorup National Park (Yalgorup NP). Some very badly affected areas of the National Park have virtually no living Tuart trees; in others up to one third of the trees are dead (CALM 2000). Most of the trees affected were the older, more mature ones'.[22] At Yalgorup, many remaining tuarts have stark grey upper branches; dead wood forks skyward like inverted lightening or broken arms of a ruined clock. As emptying skies and seas return to their original unwritten blue, they tell us catalogues of birds and creatures are vanishing.

Scientists have now identified the dieback species *Phytophthora multivora*; tuarts were thought to be resistant to the pathogen and nobody really knows why they became susceptible. 'The observation that in most cases decline cannot be attributed to a single cause is, in fact, a widely held opinion'.[23] Is it something we did or is it a natural cycle? Have we tried to fix things without fully understanding the ecological consequences of our so-called solutions? Galliano wonders if maybe the trees are dying because our activities have become separated from issues of survival.

At the thrombolite reef, Western scientific knowledge and Indigenous wisdom concur: the microbialites – the Woggaal Noorook – are precious markers of life's origins. And we agree: they are threatened by our way of life,[24] though as with the wider debate on climate change, there is no consensus on what constitutes the danger, what ought to be done about it, or by whom.

While we try to reach conclusions about our impact on the thrombolites, they silently mark time at the threshold of living and dying. The immediacy of the threat to their precarious existence, in contrast to the ancient, living lineage they represent, is a potent metaphor for our time. But because this landscape has also kept them alive for thousands of years, I think of it as a place of hope. With the help of the threshold guardians, Yalgorup has encouraged me to recover my sense of place and shown me how caring for country carries us further together, than we could go on our own.

Like every story at Yalgorup, mine has water running through it, sweet and salt, in drought or inundation, above and underground: I'm estuarine, bi-cultural by nature and circumstance. Like the fresh water which seeps from springs and collects deeper down, I've arrived after a long journey. The salt was always in my veins. I am at home here.

The waters of Yalgorup wend their way home through a catchment sprawling over hundreds of kilometres, from as far inland as Williams. Run-off soaks the wetland's mudflats and is filtered through its salt-marsh reeds. In winter during the Noongar seasons of Makuru and Djilba, when rain dilutes a lake's salinity, a thin lens of sweet water rests on the heavier, salty layer.

This lacustrine syntax is repeated in the underworld of limestone aquifers. Tree roots reach for the fresh water that floats at the top of the water table.

This terrain through which water flows is folded and layered, so that coming upon a lake or pool has something mysterious about it, a sense of discovery or revelation. This accords with a belief held by most traditional cultures, that life-sustaining water bodies – rivers and wells, fjords, billabongs and brooks, lakes and inlets – have special significance. They are boundaries, and as Martin Heidegger observed, 'a boundary is not that at which something stops, but that from which something begins its presencing'.[25] Thousands of years ago, Yalgorup's traditional Noongar owners, the Bindjareb people, founded a culture on this understanding. They learnt it from country. We can too.

This essay was awarded the inaugural prize for a nature essay by The Nature Conservancy Australia 2010–11. It was first published in *Indigo*, vol. 6, February 2011.

1   Annamaria Weldon, 'Many rivers', *dotdotdash*, vol.4, 2010.

2   In 1990 Yalgorup was added to the Ramsar Convention's 'List of Wetlands of International Importance'.

3   K. J. McNamara, 'Stromatolites – the ultimate living fossils', in *Australian Natural History* vol. 22, no. 10, 1988, pp. 476–80; R. Luu et al., 'Thrombolite (stromatolite-like microbialite) community of a coastal brackish lake (Lake Clifton) interim recovery plan no. 153 2004–2009', Western Australian Department of Conservation and Land Management, Perth, 2004.

4   M. Findlay, 'Understanding place through narrative', in *Making Sense of Place*, National Museum of Australia, Canberra 2009, p 13.

5   Thrombolite fossil shown to me by Dr Kath Grey, Chief Palaeontologist at the Geological Survey of Western Australia, Department of Mines and Petroleum.

6   George Walley, a leader and cultural teacher in the Bindjareb Noongar community, musician and historian.

7   The Herron family were graziers who lived on the coast at Lake Clifton. 'A boating accident occurred on Tuesday the 14th of December, 1886. Robert, Rachel, Anne and Sarah (Isabella was away in Bunbury at the time) went out sailing on Lake Clifton, although none could swim. Robert fell overboard, and the boat upturned. Anne and Rachel both drowned, whilst Robert and Sarah managed to cling on to the boat for two days before they were able to drift back to shore. The verdict was given as accidental drowning…' R. Richards, *The Herron Family: a history*, 1998, available via www.mandurahcommunitymuseum. org. See also: *The West Australian*, 30 December 1886.

8   Edward Relph, 'A pragmatic sense of place', in *Making Sense of Place*, National Museum of Australia, Canberra, 2008, part 4, p. 318.

9   Naturalist Laurie Smith, an Adaptation Resident 2009–10 at SymbioticA UWA, was joint collaborator with the author on 'Sharing the edge' (a creative, research and community arts project based on Lake Clifton) during their residencies.

10 Sanskrit word meaning an 'oblation' or 'gift from god'; blessed food given and received after a ceremony.

11   J. Baudrillard, quoted by Dr Paul Thomas in 'Stillness: arts, science and technology', Director's Statement, John Curtin Gallery, Biennale of Electronic Arts Perth, 2007.

12   John Shaw Neilson, 'The crane is my neighbour' originally published in *Beauty Imposes*, Angus & Robertson, Melbourne, 1938; I read it more recently in *Collected verse of John Shaw Neilson* ed. Margaret Roberts, UWA Publishing Perth, WA, 2012, p. 412.

13   B. Farmer, *The Bone House*, Giramondo, Artarmon, NSW, 2005, p. 10.

14   Although you'd never know it, these dull rocks swarm with life, with an estimated (well, obviously estimated) three billion individual organisms on every square yard of rock. Sometimes, when you look carefully, you can see tiny strings of bubbles rising to the surface as they give up their oxygen. In two billion years such tiny exertions raised the level of oxygen in the Earth's atmosphere to twenty per cent, preparing the way for the next, more complex, chapter in life's history. B. Bryson *A Short History of Nearly Everything* Doubleday, Canada, 2012.

15   L.S. Moore, B. Knott and N. F. Stanley, 'The stromatolites of Lake Clifton', *Western Australia Search*, vol. 14, 1984, pp. 309–14.

16   L. Moore, cited in *Stromatolites* by McNamara, K. J.: the dominant filamentous cyanobacterium, scytonema, forms the mineral aragonite from calcium carbonate in a photosynthetic process fed by upwelling groundwater that is rich in calcium bicarbonate.

17   K.J. McNamara, *Stromatolites*, Revised edition, Western Australian Museum, Perth, 2009, p. 8.

18   George Walley, personal conversation, Fremantle Arts Centre, August 2009.

19   D. James, 'An Anangu ontology of place' in *Making Sense of Place*, National Museum of Australia, Canberra ACT, 2008, p. 109.

20   R. McDonald, *The Tree in Changing Light*, Random House/Knopf, NSW, 2001, p. 66.

21   G. & N. Fardin, submission to *Environmental Protection Bulletin* no. 4 Strategic Advice – Dawesville to Binningup, May 2009.

22   B. J. Keighery and V. M. Longman (Eds), *Tuart (Eucalyptus gomphocephala) and Tuart Communities*, Perth Branch Wildflower Society of Western Australia (Inc.), Nedlands, Western Australia, 2002, pp. 298–300.

23   ibid., p. 300.

24   The thrombolite (microbialite) community of the coastal brackish lake (Lake Clifton) was listed as critically endangered under the *Environment Protection and Biodiversity Conservation Act 1999* (EPBC Act) on 7 January 2010

25   M. Heidegger, 'Building dwelling thinking' (from *Poetry, Language, Thought*, translated by Albert Hofstadter, Harper Colophon Books, New York, 1971), quoted by Kit Wise from the Faculty of Art and Design, Monash University in 'Presencing nature', *Walk Catalogue*, National Exhibition Touring Support (NETS), Victoria, 2009.

NATURE NOTES
the memory of earth – Noongar seasons

Under eucalypt branches, the white threads
of stamen stitch tannin water, but this
Kambarang sunlight is leaded with shades...[1]

BIRAK, December and January

Thousands of black swans and shelducks flock to
Lake Pollard, where the surface is covered by an
impressive array of birds. On windy days, lines of
swans float up and down, carried along by opposing
wind-generated currents. Their silhouettes, stark
against sun-struck water, create a massive, moving
sculpture. There are times when almost all the swans
trumpet at the same time, the sounds blending like
an orchestra and choir.

Extreme summer heat accelerates evaporation from
Yalgorup's lakes. At Lake Clifton, the thrombolite
reef becomes exposed and sun-bleached. Yalgorup's
wetlands were once a food source for the Bindjareb
Noongar people who collected freshwater crayfish,
<u>marron</u>, frogs and <u>turtle</u> there. Its dense tree cover

42 *marron – Cherax tenuimanus, marrin in Noongar*
long-necked turtle – Chelodina oblonga, Yakkan/
Yakkinn/Ya-gyne/Yarkan – alternative
spellings in Noongar

provided habitat for the <u>possum</u> they hunted. Noongar
diet included the seeds of the <u>cycad palm,</u> which has
many Indigenous names – bayu or by-yu in the South
West, and the seeds known as kwinin; as early as
1846, Moore[2] recorded the name djiri for macrozamia,
noting its poisonous natural state (which we now know
is due to the presence of the toxin macrozamin) and
the elaborate Indigenous method of de-toxification.
I am here paraphrasing a longer, lyrical account by
West Australian contemporary botanical poet John
C. Ryan[3] in which he traces macrozamia's 'multiple
narrative streams including poetic, scientific and
Aboriginal knowledge' observing that 'The complexity
of Noongar vocabulary surrounding Zamia signifies
its cultural importance as a foodstuff.' Various wattle
and banksia blossoms and roots provided spices or
supplementary foods, and bulrush rhizomes were
ground and baked into 'cakes'.

*Western ringtail possum – Pseudocherus
occidentalis, koomal in Noongar
cycad palm – Macrozamia riedlei*

BUNURU, February and March

Water-filtering <u>rushes</u> and sedges turn silver, less and less green fringes the shores. The waterline recedes. Wherever the sandy edges of a lake have remained damp at this time of year, it is a sign of freshwater seeps. Because there is almost no rain, the tracks of <u>bandicoots,</u> foxes, rabbits and shoreline birds are well preserved, pressed into softer ground and sun-baked, like hieroglyphs in clay. Even long-necked turtle tracks may sometimes be seen on the sandy bed of shallow pools which are fed from seeps.

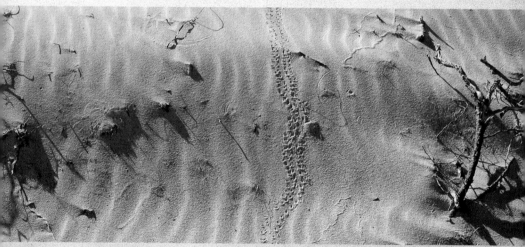

bulrush – Typha domingensis
bandicoots – Isoodon obesulus,
kwenda in Noongar

At Lake Clifton and at most of Yalgorup's lakes, white foam often appears at the edges, piled up by the prevailing wind. It is caused by organic processes, and is not a sign of detergents. However, concentrations in the nutrient levels of the lakes become more apparent in bunuru, because heat triggers algal activity (which *is* increased by the presence of nutrients). Researchers have recorded that an apparent increase in nutrient levels in the lake may have caused an increase in the amount of the epiphyte *Cladophora*. In 1988 *Cladophora* was noted to cover microbialites in late spring and summer but the growth was sufficiently light to be removed during autumn and winter through wind-generated wave action. Further phosphate input into Lake Clifton may result in further increase of *Cladophora*, which would inevitably inhibit the formation of microbialites.[4]

For two consecutive years, I found large fragments of benthic mat stranded in between the thrombolites,

where it had been washed into shallows near the viewing platform. It is thought that this algal mat had lifted from the deeper lake bed and broken up during the hot months, possibly as a result of decomposition of the lower layers of the mat by bacterial activity, followed by dislodgment during storms.[5]

Late bunuru is when graceful sun-moths hatch. They only fly during a four-week period, and this is when you might see brilliant flashes of their orange underwings, small as airborne postage stamps, fluttering low through the mat-rushes. This moth

46   *graceful sun-moth – Synemon gratiosa*

feeds and breeds on *Lomandra maritima*, and the same plant's roots host burrowing larvae underground for one to two years.

DJERAN, April and May

Cooling south-west winds bring relief from the summer heat and when the rain comes, petrichor, the smell of rain on warm rock, fills Yalgorup. During the hot season, eucalypt oil evaporates from the leaves, then settles on the bark and rocks of the park. When the first rain falls, chemical interaction between water and this oily coating releases the characteristically pungent smell.

Some of my best photos of the wetlands were taken in Djeran, when the water level is rising again and brilliant calm days create attractive reflections and light effects.

At this time of year waders can still forage in the shallows, so I have photographed many small birds,

as well as swans, egrets and white-faced herons, just offshore. This was also the season when group fishing in lakes and estuaries took place. Food was abundant, and the Bindjareb women undertook gathering of edible bulbs and seeds.

I witnessed a curious phenomenon in mid-Djeran at Lake Clifton: midge swarms ascending from the fringing trees, clearly visible as hundreds of dark columns, twisting upwards into clear sky. Viewed from my vantage point far out on the platform, the curling wisps resembled smoke. Ominous, in a place where bushfire is a constant hazard – however, the buzzing of

48   swan – *Cygnus atratus*; *Gooljak/Kooljak, Weela*
little egret – *Egretta garzetta*
white-faced heron – *Egretta novaehollandiae*

insects was unmistakeable, and soon confirmation came in the form of a small flock when welcome swallows and tree martins perched all around me on the timber rails, their stomachs distended by this hearty breakfast.

Prescribed burns, an attempt to manage the fire danger, recommence now unless the weather is prohibitive. Real smoke from Pinjarra drifting over Lake Clifton creates interesting photographic effects – the landscape can look as subtly shaded as Japanese watercolour.

Splendid fairy-wrens fly along the bush trail by the lake, in social and family groups. And there's fruit on the Apple of Sodom weeds which unfortunately still infest lakeside properties along the track south of the viewing platform, as does the narrow-leaf cotton bush with the hair-like filling of seed pods bursting just about now. I soon learn that both of these fascinating and attractive plants are noxious weeds and forbidden fruits that invade and threaten indigenous vegetation.

welcome swallow — Hirundo neoxena
tree martin — Petrochelidon nigricans
splendid fairy wren — Malurus splendens
Apple of Sodom — Solanum linneanum
narrow-leaf cotton bush — Gomphocarpus fruticosus

MAKURU, June and July

The days are shorter, the air much colder; gales are frequent and rainfall more consistent. The landscape palette around the lake changes. Summer's intense blue skies and water, its bleached, dry shoreline now give way to the paler blues and cloudy greys reflected in filling rock pools and soaked ground. The Bindjareb people were kept warm by smouldering banksia branches with giant seed-pod glowing like a coal, held under their skin cloaks (booka).

The white-faced heron knows the refilled rock-pools are a source of food. I've spent hours watching this bird 'fish' and even longer writing poems about it.

Along the lakeside trail, minute white fungi are growing on dead stumps, moss covers the rocks and lichen is spreading over tree limbs. Just after sunrise, at Lake Hayward, I saw a magnificent pair of forest red-tailed black cockatoos – karak – perched high in a tuart tree. Later that morning I photographed great spreads of orange fungi growing in grassy ground near Martins Tank.

DJILBA, August and September

Pink fairy orchids grow abundantly around the Old Kiln, and they soften this abandoned site. They are by no means the only wildflowers growing at Yalgorup, and more than fifty are listed for enthusiasts at the Lake Preston Wildflower Walk off Caves Road near Lake Preston.[6]

Galls are growing on the trees, there are more fungi, and I've found intricate hammocked webs of the giant sac spider slung in the sedges by the lakeside

pink fairy orchid – Caladinia latifolia
giant sac spider – Miturga agelenina

trail. These spider 'retreats' can be as large as an adult's hand. Their design is architectural, reminiscent of the Sydney Opera House, with brilliant white sheets of silk anchored to the sedge at various points, looking distinctly geometrical.

Kookaburras swoop and blue wrens chatter to distract me from their nests as I walk on the lakeside trail. A heron flies past my shoulder while I am on the viewing platform, and I feel the draught of its wings on my neck.

The Bindjareb people hunted <u>emu</u>, <u>kangaroo</u>, bandicoot and possum during this warming season.

Just up from the waterline at Lake Pollard, <u>samphires</u> are turning from emerald to ruby. At Lake Hayward, <u>cut-leaf hibbertias</u> and <u>stalked guinea flowers</u> are beginning to flower, and native cherry or <u>broom ballart</u> hangs in glassy globes like pale red grapes. <u>Donkey orchids</u> are out at Lake Preston. At the nearby ocean beach of Preston, dune vegetation (which has held the sand fast against winter winds) remains bright green.

At Lake Clifton, water is still rising above the thrombolites, which by now are completely inundated. On very calm days, out on the platform I have looked down into clear water and photographed schools of tiny fingerlings swimming around them.

emu — wetj; Dromaius novaehollandiae
kangaroo — Macropus fuliginosus; yongka
samphire — Halosarcia indica, H. halocnemoides
    cut-leaf hibbertia — Hibbertia cuneiformis
stalked guinea flowers — Hibbertia racemosa
broom ballart — Exocarpos sparteus
    donkey orchid — Diurus corymbosa

53

KAMBARANG, October and November

The heat has begun in earnest on the South West coast, bringing out wildflowers, mosquitos and snakes waking from hibernation. Mid-afternoon, walking inland to the Yalgorup lakes from Preston Beach, I almost step on a sluggish dugite, warming itself on the verge of a bush track. It is so sleepy that I spend a long time photographing its beautiful black and ochre body markings, and in the process of admiring it, overcome any fear. The same afternoon, I find feral bees swarming in the hollow of an ancient

54 dugite — *Pseudonaja affinis*;
          kabarda in Noongar

tuart. These bees displace nesting black cockatoos, whose habitat is being decimated by urban sprawl, tree felling and feral invasions.

At north Lake Preston I try to photograph the largest mob of kangaroo that I have ever seen, but they are too fast, on the move across an empty paddock.

At Lake Clifton there is a delicate web of late-flowering clematis with spidery, cream petals, strung over a barbed wire fence. The bush is full of contrasts – delicate climbers with intricate growing habits alongside the sculptural swamp banksia, which are also in full colour now.

Clear sky brings the opportunity of photographing a full moon reflected in Lake Clifton as it rises over still-submerged thrombolites, which appear to glow in its light. This unforgettable night will find its way into my essays and poems; there's a thrill in witnessing life after dark, off the beaten track, a sense of magic which makes it easy to understand why this lake and its living

clematis – Clematis pubescens
swamp banksia – Banksia littoralis

rocks are so significant to Noongar culture.

Turtles, frogs and crayfish were hunted by the Indigenous people in Kambarang, as they began moving towards the coast where they would spend the warmer months. The 1834 slaughter of so many Bindjareb people whose totem was the turtle (long-necked) led to near-starvation for the survivors when, in the absence of turtle totem-holders, hunting for this essential staple became taboo. Fortunately in this season yams and bird eggs abounded, and it was still possible to trap possum and kangaroo.

1   Annamaria Weldon, 'The memory of earth', *Westerly*, vol. 56, no. 1, July 2010, pp. 96–7.

2   G. F. Moore, (1846), *Diary of ten years eventful life of an early settler in Western Australia* and also *Descriptive vocabulary of the language in common use amongst the Aborigines of Western Australia*, UWA Press, Nedlands, 1978.

3   John Charles Ryan, *Green Sense*, Trueheart academic, Oxford, 2012, pp. 75–7.

4   L. S. Moore and I. V. Turner, (1988). 'Stable isotopic, hydrogeochemical and nutrient aspects of lake – groundwater relations at Lake Clifton', in G. Lowe (ed), *Proceedings of Swan Coastal Plain Groundwater Management Conference*, Western Australian Water Resources Council, 1999, pp. 201–13, cited in 'Lake Clifton', *Yalgorup National Park Management Plan 1995–2005*, p. 40, <www.dec.wa.gov.au/pdf/nature/management/yalgorup.pdf>.

5   Jennifer Alexander, 'The microbial communities of Lake Clifton', essay in *Adaptation Catalogue* supporting the exhibition 'Adaptation' (first shown at INQB8 Centre for Contempoary Art, Mandurah, Western Australia May 2012 and touring until 2015), published by SymbioticA 2012, pp. 8, 9.

6   The Wildflower Walk begins at the information bay on Preston Beach Road on the corner of Caves Road in Yalgorup National Park, Lake Clifton Herron Progress and Sporting Association Inc., 2012.

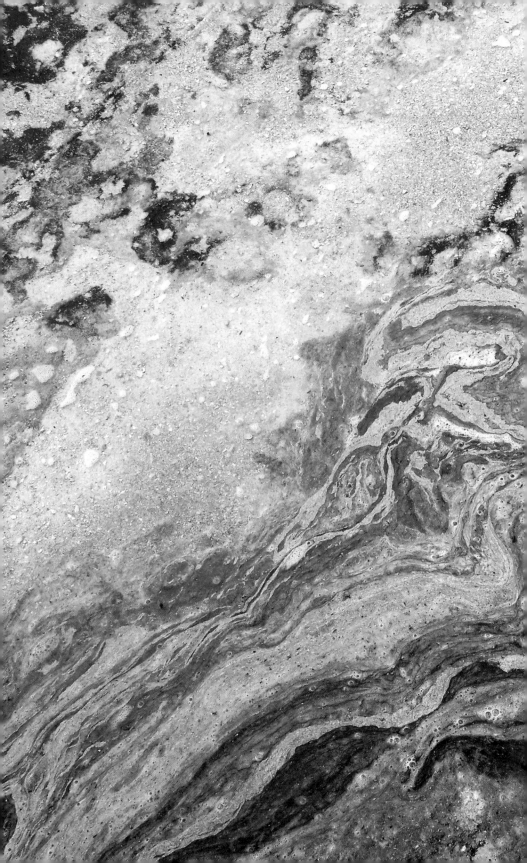

A DELICATE SEAM
– a memoir of love, loss and nature-writing

*'Sorí simensar sí men' – we are all one: all who are with us
are ourselves.*[1]

Before migrating to Western Australia I was viscerally
connected to my birth land. Wherever I was and at any
time of the day or year, I relied on an unwritten map:
it was inner, three-dimensional and haptic. I *felt* where
I was, the way we're aware if we are standing upright
or lying down, of our location at any given moment
when in our own house. I had a tactile sense of Malta's
position as the main island of an archipelago, and I
had such a connection to those rocky fragments that I
appreciated where they were situated in relation to each
other and the neighbouring Mediterranean coastlines.

In Malta, through an accumulation of particulars
which radiated beyond the horizon (and perhaps began
their imprint even before I was born), I could read
the island fluently and knew – still know, whenever
I return – every place. I don't mean merely that I
recognise their names, but my profoundly geographic
sense of them. From any town, village or hillside, I can
picture the nearest coast's intimate details – whether it
banks gently down to aqua shallows in bare limestone
flanks, or falls sheer: high, chalky cliffs festooned with
caper bushes, crumbling to shadowy, shale slopes and
wine-dark water.

60

It's embodied, it's ancestral: islanders understand the geology of the ground beneath their feet through stories still handed down from a time when survival depended on knowing the ways it's seasonally irrigated; all the winds and gales to which it's exposed; how their litany of names begins. In Malta it was '*xlokk, grigal, majjistral*'. On waking each morning, before opening my eyes, the clarity of bells pealing in the next village or the feel of sheets damp with humidity would tell me if the weather was coming from nearby Sicily or from Libya, which lies to the south. At day's end, wherever I was, I anticipated the exact spot on the horizon where the sun would set. I read my island in eight directions and even blindfolded, could have told you which valley we were in by the textures of its rocks and soil, the scents of wild mignonette and orange blossom, or those subtle gradations of salt-tang on a breeze which sharpens from creek to open sea.

I no longer live in that landscape, the ground of my writing. At the age of thirty-four I moved to Western Australia. Just before I left, my first poetry collection had been published and favourably reviewed. I was described as 'obsessed with the natural world and primeval elements of her familiar Maltese landscape'. In Perth, though I continued to work as a journalist, my creative writing withered. The 'nature' in nature writing comes before the 'writing', and in this unknown land I was environmentally illiterate, bereft of my former connection to country and sense of place which had bound me to my island and inspired my poetry.

I needed a long apprenticeship to Western Australia, and more than that, to a specific local place *and to those who read it as a poem*. Unfortunately, as it is for so many migrants, our first decade here was hard work and we spent our rare recreational time with other Maltese Australians. Years were to pass before I would meet the guides to come, those who knew the layered implications of endemicity.

I had taken such guidance for granted in Malta, where my mother and grandmother passed on island lore in the course of daily life. We would talk about growing seasons and crop cycles while gardening or planning and preparing meals. There was hardly any division between countryside and towns, and the mild Mediterranean climate made us all outdoors people. The habits of the few hardy, local trees (carob, fig) or idiosyncratic details of place (like the desolate hilltop that was always perfumed with wild narcissus on Good Friday) were linked to our favourite family picnic places *and* the religious calendar. Whether you loved or loathed the popular local sport of shooting birds, you knew that migrating waterfowl flew over Comino Channel after Easter. The influential birdwatcher journal *Wingspan* describes the archipelago as 'a vital migratory stopover, but also a notorious killing field. Maltese hunters are allowed to legally shoot a few species, but in practice every bird within range is fair game'.[2] So in autumn I waited and watched as migrant raptors reached the ridges and high cliffs of the western coast.

In late summer, from August to October, the Maltese feast on fish they call lampuki, (known elsewhere as mahi–mahi, dorado or dolphin fish). Large schools find shelter from the fierce sun under rafts which fishermen make from palm fronds, then tow far offshore in calm weather: a canny method of entrapment learned by generations of fisher folk.

In Malta's valleys, along with the surround-sound of crickets and anguished braying of donkeys, there's the familiar creak of rickety windmills, which I was told had been introduced to the island early last century by a migrant returning from Australia.

My blood ran soil, as a student of mine once put it, but until I moved away I was unaware how vital that was to my creativity. In Western Australia, though I marvelled at the diversity, scale and beauty of the landscapes, I nursed a profound disorientation. Fourteen years would pass before I sent another poem to be published.

Gradually I discovered how commonplace it is, this sense of loss. Here on the west coast, our backstory is country many of us hardly know, even though land is a powerful presence in our poetry and fiction, visual arts, music and biographies. From pre-settlement sagas to the seismology of the stock exchange, land features in almost every conversation or story about family roots, social justice, the economy, art, agriculture, tourism, weather and wellbeing. We live with exceptional biodiversity, at the convergence of dramatic geological time scales. But do we really understand our great ecosystems, or their kingdoms and creatures? Half of the people living in Australia were either not born here or have a parent who was not born here; many others, Indigenous and non-indigenous, have also been separated from their Australian birth landscapes; it's unsurprising that so many are wary of forming another deep attachment to place. *I was*, and each time I relate my own experiences in public, several people from the audience seek me out to tell me that it is their story too. Often there are tears as they reveal a longing to recover that intimacy which a sense of place engenders – and reflect on how long it has been absent, a part of themselves buried when they settled instead for a marriage of convenience with their new country. My connection – or is it reconnection? – to country gives them hope that after loss, we *can* love again.

My turning point was a creative writing residency with 'Adaptation', an environmental project hosted by SymbioticA, centre of excellence in biological arts at the University of Western Australia and based at Lake Clifton in Yalgorup National Park, south of Mandurah. I worked closely with naturalist Laurie Smith on our collaborative project *Sharing the Edge*, research and text which led me to ongoing outreach work in community art projects and education. It was the first time that I'd associated with artists, scientists and local groups whose activities were focused on the complex interactions of a rich ecosystem, in one specific setting, over a three-year period.

After years of acknowledging my Adaptation artist residency as the creative catalyst for my nature writing, that reference trips off my tongue. Now I want to pause, reflect on what it has meant to me. How transforming it has been to explore Yalgorup in the company of other SymbioticA residents, including visiting scholars, with their conversations about its geology, botany, cultural history, hydrology; to be invited to join a hunt for the rare graceful sun-moth, or seed-gathering for a project to propagate the park's endemic tuarts, which are endangered by dieback; to listen for the singular music of a lone frog as I walked through the sifted light of the lake's fringing peppermint trees; to learn from impassioned bio-artists, wildflower enthusiasts and birdwatchers, proactive conservationists who can name the surrounding flora and fauna.

And so I began to learn the nature of this country the way I would learn about another culture: out of love for its language and history; because I'm drawn to the life in its landscapes, because we seem to complete something in each other and, especially in its dark material, what García Lorca termed the 'duende',[3] we come to know the truth of our lives more fully. For at Yalgorup, life often suffers: the forecasts are dark and the vulnerable imperilled.

Among the souvenirs of a Catholic education, the catechism answer to 'why are we here?' still haunts me (which of course was the purpose of learning by rote). Although I have since substituted my own understanding for many words in the official text, as a child I chanted that we are here 'to know, love and serve God in this life and be with Him in the next'. And that link between *knowing* and *loving* and *serving*, in my experience of this habitat, seems so true.

Late in the Noongar season of Bunuru, one hot March morning, I walked the dunes looking for rare, endangered graceful sun-moths (*Synemon gratiosa*) in the company of Brett Brenchley[4] from the World Wildlife Fund, now known as WWF–Australia. He told me this autumn-flying species, with bright orange underwings, typically appears across a four-to-six-week period each year. The adult moth survives from four to ten days. Despite this slim chance of a sighting, even in our target area where the moth is known to occur, we saw one. Brilliantly coloured and small as an airborne postage stamp, it fluttered low through the mat-rushes on which it feeds and breeds: *Lomandra maritima*, whose roots host burrowing larvae underground for one to two years. At rest, when folded wings concealed its fluoro-orange colouring, the motionless body was camouflaged among twigs and leaf litter. It took us three hours to find two more. I lay in the sand to photograph them, unaware I was collecting a cargo of minute larval kangaroo ticks (*Amblyomma triguttatum*), colloquially known as pepper ticks. How those bites itched, and the torment lasted for weeks…

But physical discomfort of one kind or another is part of getting to know any wild place. During Kambarang, chilled by the spring twilight, I've waited on the viewing platform for a full moon to rise above Lake Clifton. Long before it did, tree martins (*Hirundo nigricans*) and welcome swallows (*Hirundo neoxena*) flew in to roost on the timber beams below me, piping and swooping to catch a feed of insects. As the salt-marsh gave up its heat, sodden earth turned the night air pungent. And then the moon rose. As its reflection swam among the thrombolites, those pale, round rocks glowed underwater like white flowers blooming beneath black glass.

The thrombolites are a colony of 'living fossils', ancient microbialites so fragile and rare that in 2010 the Lake Clifton colony was listed as 'critically endangered' under the *Environment Protection and Biodiversity Conservation Act 1999* (EPBC Act) by the then Federal Minister for the Environment, Peter Garrett. They are the focus of 'Adaptation', which follows on from the pioneering research of Dr Linda Moore and Dr Robert Burne, who described thrombolites as 'organo-sedimentary structures that are formed by benthic microbial communities which trap and bind detrital sediment and/or precipitate calcium carbonate'.[5]

Because oxygen is a by-product of their photosynthesis, thrombolites and stromatolites (which once covered much of the earth's surface) are thought to have raised the planet's atmospheric concentration of oxygen, eventually enabling other life forms to flourish.

There's such an obvious correlation between this hypothesis of western science and the Bindjareb

Noongar traditions: Yalgorup's first people regard the thrombolites as *the living presence* of Yalgorup's creation story. Cultural teacher George Walley told me that in his traditional language the thrombolites are known as Woggaal Noorook, eggs which the rainbow serpent laid as she travelled south. George wants Yalgorup's stories to be understood and retold. To retell them well, as part of narrating the story of such places, is the work of custodians of the land and of nature writers, poets of place, listeners to country. While habitats disappear, extinctions accelerate, languages and traditions die, storytellers recover the remnants and draw attention to what is no longer there.

Like most writers, my reading habit is obsessive and extensive – other nature writers' essays, landscape memoirs, poetry, libraries of reference books! Those who have written about a country's hidden or overlooked life, the memoir of its forgotten aspects, have changed my regard for places I once took for granted, or had never fully discovered. Like the time I've spent with Yalgorup's original texts – its rocks, trees, lakes and ridges – these readings have been sojourns of the body and the soul, as much as of the mind.

And now, at every glimpse of the wetland's tenacious complexity I feel that I am being asked: Will you witness this? Will it get under your skin, like the pepper ticks, and can you say how that feels? When living rocks glow underwater at full moon, is it science or the poetics of light? If you write it, will it emerge as the same truth, speaking many different languages: geology tracing thrombolites back to first life, poetry beguiling the senses beyond our limited sense of time and possibility, the Bindjareb Noongar tradition wisely saying they were there 'in the beginning?'

My Maltese attunement and sense-memories included the sharp, sherbet taste of oxalis stems, which we children used to pull from the roadside and chew; the comforting heat of my school playground's dry-stone wall at lunch recess in winter on a sunny day, as warm against my bare legs as a loaf fresh from the oven; the summer scent of pine needles, rosemary and geraniums in my grandpa's country garden. And today, Yalgorup too is more than a name and map location to me, it is a sensory smorgasbord – there are the savoury-citrus notes on biting freshly picked marsh samphire, and pungent, earthy petrichor inhaled when first rains wash eucalypt oils from the rocks and ground. After a long trek, I often seek the comforting strength and smoothness of a paperbark trunk to support my back as I sit with my feet cooling in the lake. And always, there's the discourse of birds: the particularly social songs of grey fantails and splendid fairy-wrens, the trumpeting of swans, together with the crickets and midges, frogs and the shushing of wind through casuarina (swamp sheoak *Allocasuarina obesa*) trees. All things conversing as they create each moment's ephemeral sonar map.

From the changing colour palette of its seasons to the way ground hardens in summer and softens with seepage in the wet season, I know Yalgorup as a dynamic, living and breathing place. I feel it knows me, too. This *knowing* has nurtured my sense of belonging there, my awe of the endemic, and a growing susceptibility to the nuances of wetland.

In the years I have been visiting, studying, photographing, writing about and collaborating on art projects at Yalgorup, I've observed how my relationship with this region has nothing to do with epic scale, nor with European ideals of beauty. I'm from a small island, so such a contained ecosystem (relative to many other Australian landscapes) appeals to me. But it isn't immediately endearing country, this wild and narrow coastal strip folding many lakes and stories into 13,000 hectares of tuart woodlands, coastal heath, paperbark and sedge swamps. Nevertheless, the seasons I spent at Yalgorup reawakened my dormant sensitivity to landscape, and revealed a tissue of stories as layered as its swamp paperbarks.

Teeming with life, this ecosystem is so vital to the survival of endemic and migratory birds that in 1990 Yalgorup was added to the Ramsar List of Wetlands of International Importance.[6] My natural curiosity and many, many issues around 'belonging' led me past the thrombolites into the unobserved worlds at the rims of lakes and dunes, on the edges of ocean, land and estuary. It drew me to their intimacies, which I found intriguing, and as wonderfully distracting as notes scribbled in the margins of a library book.

There's a cascade of losses – personal, creative, communal – when the place in which you live is not the place you love, when it's a marriage of convenience with the landscape instead of reciprocal intimacy. Like a love-marriage, cherished country calls you to physical proximity and is a creative relationship sustained and nourished by community involvement. Through my deepening relationship with this place of swamps, and through sharing my appreciation for the patterns, particularities and life history of this wild coastal strip, I began to write myself home. In doing so I seem to have helped others towards a new appreciation of their surroundings, or (so often this must come first) their own lost sense of place.

When I lived in Malta, the island where I was born, I took it for granted that the land loved me right back, just as I never doubted that the country knew I was there. The complex connection of a migrant to their native landscape is something which I believe we don't speak about enough; it is too often misinterpreted as sentimentality, quickly dismissed as backwards looking, or heard as a failure to appreciate the adopted country's many blessings, even 'un-Australian'. What I'm referring to is none of these: it is a physical and psychic attunement to place, the accretion of instinctual and learned knowledge which arises from and continually affirms a sense of belonging. And this is not something we can come to alone, but from within a community of connected souls, a community we may have to find for ourselves.

My poet's response to nature now includes collaborative projects which have merged my texts to dance, to music and sculpture and images. Drawing on my love for Yalgorup and my wanderings through its landscape, I've held journal workshops in women's shelters and taken young writers with disabilities and their carers out on field trips, before exploring the alchemy of writing about our encounters. Sometimes we've enjoyed the company of Bindjareb Noongar cultural teacher George Walley, who has given generous guidance and permission to pass on language words and stories.

All of this is process, the backstory behind the artefacts which result – poems, essays, photos. It is also known as living – or a way of life, one which has changed me, slowed me down. In appreciating the thrombolites' glacial rate of growth and their unceasing creativity, I've discovered renewed connection to my own ways of 'making', whether that is poems or relationships. I have returned to a deep participation with the land and its communities.

The source of this transformation remains a mystery to me, and if I were asked about my beliefs and ontology, I'd say I am happy to live with the unknowing. A poet's work isn't to explain it but, as the late John O'Donohue said 'to draw alongside the mystery as it is emerging and somehow bring it into presence and into birth'.[7] Art which draws from this true source works on me (and, I am told, on others) like the old magic of threshold rituals. It transforms my perception.

Making such art involves attending to the individuality of things, the hidden essence of their specific details, their dynamic processes and their endemic identity. Through profound attention, something *may be* called into presence – a clarity which unites bodily senses and theoretical mind. Glen Albrecht has named this feeling '*eutierria*' – where 'the boundaries between self and the rest of nature are obliterated and a deep sense of peace and connectedness pervades consciousness'. For a while, the ephemeral seems permanent, the alien acknowledged, and the anonymous known.

When I drive past Walley Bridge on the way to Mandurah, with its words of welcome in Noongar, my heart lifts and my lungs feel as though the oxygen in the air has increased. I've come to recognise these moments as thresholds, and as welcome. There are so many thresholds to cross on my way to the wetlands – water thresholds, language thresholds, the threshold of communion with creatures. I notice pelicans soaring above. A few kilometres further on, a wedgetail eagle or a hawk always flies across the freeway, just a little ahead of me. In his landscape memoir *The Blue Plateau*, Mark Tredinnick wrote that the practice of belonging begins with forgetfulness of self. When you go deep into the wild nature of your own process, there's the chance you'll glimpse something as awesome as it is fleeting. And because 'going with the flow' implies a kind of surrender (I use the term in its sense of the heart being opened, rather than vanquished), it can feel risky. But we are in need of environmental writing which risks emotional involvement and does not negate mystery, for I suspect our alienation from nature is the wound at the core of today's environmental dilemmas.

The Sanskrit word for a line of wisdom literature is *sutra*, which means 'a thread binding things together'.

In traditional cultures, stories repair and strengthen the web of life. And in contemporary life, where our understanding has become threadbare, where we ourselves have been torn away, writing darns, patches and restores the embroidery of old narratives we have almost lost. It is nature writing which has woven me into the fabric of Yalgorup country. When I followed the fleeting life cycle of graceful sun-moths, watching them flash orange through the rushes, I knew that our lives were joined at a delicate seam. If the moths disappeared from those dunes (as they have from many of their Western Australian habitats), each autumn I would feel as though part of me was missing.

I'd like to think that writing may help to save this precarious landscape, but it may not. What the literature of place can do is awaken our imaginations and gather together the scattered, vital pieces which connect one story to another. It is one name for the threads with which witnesses of place stitch and bind us to the world, our Ariadne thread back to the world within the world.

1   David Morley, 'Marriage Vows of a Rom to a Gadji' (translated from the Romani language), *The Gypsy and the Poet*, Carcanet Press, Manchester, 2013, p. 63.

2   *Wingspan*, vol. 21, no. 2, 2011, 'Birds in Focus: Conservation and Research News: Birds under fire in Maltese crossing', p. 10.

3   'Duende' is a southern Spanish word that means dwarf. I use it here connotatively, to refer to a powerfully embodied soulfulness, which equates to the 'daemon' of a place, artwork or person. At once chthonic and spiritual ('of earth and spirit'), this energy flashes forth in the midst of a performance, or finds us at particular portals in the landscape, revealing creation as sentient and animate.

4   Brett Brenchley is now the Coordinator, Climate Change Services at the City of Mandurah.

5   R. V. Burne, and L. S. Moore (1987). 'Microbiolites: organo sedimentary deposits of benthic microbial communities', *Palaios*, vol. 2, 1987, pp. 241–54.

6   Convention on Wetlands of International Importance especially as Waterfowl Habitat. Ramsar (Iran), 2 February 1971, UN Treaty Series No. 14583. Peel-Yalgorup system was added on 7 June 1990.

7   John O'Donohue, interviewed by Krista Tippett, *On Being*, American Public Radio, 2008, transcript, viewed 10 July 2013, <www.onbeing.org/program/inner-landscape-beauty/transcript/2427>.

NATURE NOTES
sharing the edge

*Where is an edge – a dangerous edge – and where is the trail to
the edge and the strength to climb it?*[1]

In the beginning, I thought Yalgorup National Park was
an impoverished landscape, shouldered on limestone
ridges, its depressions and swales mantled in wind-
scoured shrubs. The low-lying, sedge-fringed littorals
of interdunal lakes seemed to be lost in a nowhere land,
an empty strand between estuary and ocean (rather
than hidden, an adjective frequently used to describe
this lake system). But it is not empty: there are ten
lakes, sanctuary to thousands of migratory birds, who
depend on these ideal wading grounds for survival
after arduous flights from the north. Yalgorup's water

bodies are pooled among coastal dunes. Their water recedes in the summer months. Each winter they fill with rain, with run-off and seepage from springs. And the Southern Hemisphere's largest reef of critically endangered thrombolites survives at Lake Clifton. Elsewhere, most thrombolites can no longer be referred to as living rocks, only as fossils.

In time, I came to understand that Yalgorup is neither hidden nor lost, but rather a place most people have not found. And that this may be its true condition and purpose: to be, always, an edge place on the very margin of our awareness.

There is an eternal landscape, a geography of the soul; we search for its outlines all our lives.[2]

In Maltese, the ancient Aramaic language of my birth island, Yalgorup would be described as '*imwarrab*',

81

which translates roughly as 'put away', as in rejected, shunned or discarded. I've always felt some mystery might unexpectedly be revealed at any moment in such recondite places. Perhaps because it is already here, overlooked in plain view, as Annie Dillard observed in *Pilgrim at Tinker Creek* and mythology suggests. No matter when I am at Yalgorup, I am never disappointed. A cluster of pink enamel orchids is like a visitation. Fairy-wrens, their feathers a sudden blue, angelic. In a time almost forgotten now, the liminal – waysides, verges, borderlands and boundaries – was

pink enamel orchids – *Elythranthera emarginata*
splendid fairy-wrens – *Malurus splendens*

recognised as a place of transformation, charged with energy. We observed and intuited that these borderlines are where life grows most profusely, and what is marginal fights for survival by adapting. Where creation's growing edges encounter one another and together create a new centre.

There is a great deal of unmapped country within us
which would have to be taken into account
in an explanation of our gusts and storms.[3]

Apart from the thrombolites, this 13,000 ha pinch of coast and wetland has no extreme or dramatic features. Access to its lakes is difficult. There are no scenic drives, few viewing areas which a casual visitor could get to by vehicle. The lakes are not tidal, have no river inlets, nor do they flow to the sea. The vegetation around their shores is, at first glance, unremarkable.

There are a few exceptions: a portion of Lake Preston is adjacent to its nearby townsite and tourist amenities; an viewing platform at Lake Clifton is well signposted and has a sealed road leading to its carpark, but Martins Tank is an eight-kilometre drive from the main road down corrugated, unsealed sand and gravel. I have tried driving there with a friend whose car is not an off-road vehicle, and we had to turn back for fear her engine would be shaken loose. But if you have appropriate transport, in winter this location offers lush and sheltered picnic sites, with well-maintained barbeques and, for campers, flat ground with soft grasses surrounded by enchanting woodland groves.

However, the wilder majority of the park demands determined trekking from those who want to see more.

I am not a determined trekker. But I am an 'edge person', drawn to overlooked terrain, to fragile country that looks harsh, to unremarkable outlooks which, if examined in detail, often narrate rich stories of becoming. The pull of the marginal is this country's big drawcard.

A sense of place is the sixth sense, an internal compass and map made by memory and spatial perception together.[4]

I have learned Yalgorup's landscape as though it were my second language. It happened gradually. Then, one afternoon in late summer (Bunuru), walking rough ground west of Lake Preston, I felt how weary I'd become of translating what often looked familiar – but was not – into an approximation of another country:

my other country, that other country which, even
after thirty years away, determines my aesthetics:
that encoded palette of colours, textures and shapes
which attract me viscerally. Many Yalgorup vistas
evoke Malta's salt-scoured terrain, the island's sand and
coastal hills where the globergina caprock's uncannily
cranial patina, with its gouged and shadowed sockets,
lies partially exhumed in terra rossa among desolate,
wind-bowed carob trees. My school motto was
'Hewn from the Rock'. It referred to the bedrock of
the Maltese archipelago's rolling landscapes. Harder

than Yalgorup's limestone formations, when quarried for building Maltese stone weathers to the buttery gold which characterises the island's dwellings, its ancient fortifications and kilometres of bastions. Once strewn with rubble, over the centuries Malta has been transformed to cultivated land girdled by endless dry-stone walls, irrigated from subterranean aquifers via a system of stone aqueducts. And, because every islander's family history is 'land-marked', the senses of place and of identity are inseparable. And yet, I left. How long does a new homecoming take?

Homecoming, I suspect, is all about letting go of other places to embrace where you are now. A process: if you let the land in, it will work you out. That's what the Yalgorup lakes had to do, when sea water was trapped inland as ocean levels rose and fell during the last (Northern Hemisphere) ice age. Water flowed inland and back. Slowly, the coastal profile changed and water outlets were sealed off by growing coastal dunes.

Aerial views of the national park today show glassy intervals of blue, parallel to the coast: ten interdunal lakes in three long strands unfurl towards the east, catching the sun like a net for light.

When you name something you think you have seen it.[5]

Yalgorup's riches of natural history and beauty are a constant reminder that the Western lexicon, with its non-Indigenous accounts of how trees, stones, grasses, marsupials, reptiles and birds were given their names, is just one anthology in a much older library. For here,

everything has other names, names they had before, names belonging to another web, which also maps the unseen and overlooked world. Such naming may take a lifetime or more to learn.

Even so, western common names and the younger stories behind many scientific names for flora and fauna do fascinate me. I appreciate having a range of precise words and accurate names with which to bring readers into the presence of a particular landscape, just as a painter plays with a palette of pigments. An opportunity to extend my vocabulary and knowledge came at the start of my creative writing residency with Adaptation, when I worked closely with naturalist Laurie Smith. He's an acute observer and entertaining raconteur, with forty years of experience in the field and writing scientific publications, mostly through the Western Australian Museum. Our collaborative research and text project *Sharing the Edge* led to ongoing outreach work in local community art projects and education.

I couldn't have had a better introduction to the wetlands. In my site log I began to record bird descriptions, their locations, the time of day and the date when I saw or heard them, noting which were pointed out to me by Laurie and which I spotted unprompted: rock parrot, red-capped dotterel, black-winged stilts, shelducks, white-faced herons, tree martins and welcome swallows, bronzewings, brown honeyeaters,

rock parrot — *Neophema petrophila*
red-capped dotterel — *Charadrius ruficapillus*
black-winged stilts — *Himantopus himantopus*
shelducks — *Tadorna tadornoides*
bronzewings — *Phaps chalcoptera*
brown honeyeaters — *Lichmera indistincta*

90

a <u>western yellow robin,</u> <u>Carnaby's cockatoos.</u> Laurie's knowledge and interests were broad and his background knowledge often became the inspiration for a poem or essay. Even so, at Yalgorup it seemed wise to remember that English and Latin names were not the first and will not be the last words to describe what surrounds me. They are recent versions of an older storytelling.

In the sorry process of losing those older stories, we have forgotten, too, that some names have the power to reanimate. These are reasons why many traditions have rules and taboos about writing or speaking the proper names of places or learning associated rituals, often forbidden until a person has undergone a period of initiation. There is wisdom, I think, in these customs. They recognise that naming a thing or a person with quickly-assumed familiarity might incline the speaker towards false claims of ownership, or status. First, one must listen. And one must have a guide whose country this is.

western yellow robin — Eopsaltria griseogularis
Carnaby's cockatoos — Calyptorhynchus latirostris

For years now I have listened to the wetlands as though before Yalgorup there was only noise. This was not the soundtrack I'd imagined for my homecoming: a sandplain froglet repeating the same notes, like a child squelching a wet balloon in the garden of a neighbouring house, its bass line running under the piping cries of swallows. Nor was this the country I thought would bind me to another kind of kinship. Wetlands where my individual lifespan seems less than nothing, shrunk to insignificance by geologic time-scales. But sometimes now, I recognise the wingbeat of approaching black swans, or a pair of shelducks calling out a landing strip to companions

I can't see yet, who will fly in low from the south at any moment. Hearing a distant reply, I may time my lens shutter to frame a bird's virtuoso glide and skim as it alights, rippling a reflection on the expectant lake of my photograph. The gratitude I feel at such moments is not about the picture my camera has captured – it is for my sense of belonging.

Perhaps the truth depends on a walk around the lake.[6]

Martins Tank seems the calmest of lakes. Its waters have the highest salinity in Yalgorup's chain of lakes, and do not attract many birds. Sheltered by fringing paperbarks which grow down to the high-water line, the surface is almost always as glossed as a photograph. In contrast to the shoreline's textured detail – its crosshatch reed patterns, etched stones, the wild calligraphy which wading birds scrawl in the mud – Martins Tank on a still day seems mysterious and reflective as a scrying basin. The same solitary pair of ducks is always there, doing nothing, it seems, just floating far out in the centre, where the water is deepest.

On a day when its water shone like polished graphite, I photographed them landing on the lake. They flew in low and, for what seemed the longest time, skimmed just above their doubles. There is nothing else in my final print but blue-grey reflected sky and *two* pairs of ducks, one pair flying upside down. After developing hundreds of images from the wetlands, this remains my favourite. One of the things I see again and again in this picture is that nature is a doubler, creating twinned images on water, reflections of verging trees, clouds and overflying birds. It has given a bird two wings, paired it with a mate and replicated it in an egg. There is some mystery, some code of creation in this realisation. How paradoxical that we value the singular, the individual, as the highest and most potent expression of life.

We live, today, in such perpetual motion that it seems a miracle, this framing of a single moment, excised by the blink of a camera shutter from the flow of time. 'It is this stillness things dream of, it

is this stillness we dream of. It is this the cinema lingers over increasingly today, in its nostalgia for slow motion and the freeze-frame, as the highest point of drama.'[7] Is there some revelatory quality in each moment, of which we become aware only when it is chiselled out of the distracting background by high focus and cropping, and we are suddenly struck by the epiphany it frames?

Terry Tempest Williams writes passionately about her conversion to stillness in her book *Finding Beauty in a Broken World*: 'Speed is the buzz, the blur, the drug. Life out of focus becomes our way of seeing. We no longer expect clarity...We don't know how to stop'.[8] And after repeated visits to Lake Clifton's living rocks, with their thousands of years of history and a growing rate of 0.1 mm per year, I understand that transformation. Observing the thrombolites has slowed me down. In stillness, I have become more receptive to nature's sacraments, aware of its orders and anomalies, attuned to the cadence of creation. Maybe the healing of country and of spirit begins as simply as this?

Standing at the edge of north Lake Preston just before dawn, it is easy to imagine time itself has not yet begun. My camera lens draws everything closer: memory and the day, what is near and what is distant. Breath of the lake rises. Fallen bark crackles. Pelican wings beat overhead to gain the breeze. Then comes the moment – quite quickly – when, through the mist-light, a bleached palette resolves: silvered shoreline, fringing grasses' ripe seed-heads, gleams of bright water, black-and-white bands of waders (avocets, banded stilts, pied cormorants and oystercatchers and many more)

96   Avocets – *Recurvirostra novae hollandiae*
        banded stilts – *Cladorhynchus leucocephalus*
      pied cormorants – *Phalacrocorax varius*
          pied oystercatchers – *Haematopus longirostris*

out on the sandbar. As the sun rises, the light shifts
again and is soon a blaze that consumes the landscape
without burning it: after the cool monochromes of
dawn, the colours of flame and water, of chlorophyll's
viridian, jade and all the mineral and carnate world,
appear as magically as fire on the moon.

This wetland is an ark of survivors. They are
in constant communion with each other and the
surrounding earth, just like sunlight and shade, the
visible and the unseen, sound and silence. Some birds
are paired with their reflection on the luminous
shallows, other creatures are so cryptic they are only
evidenced by the signs they leave. At the end of last
winter I found a giant sac spider's delicate, woven retreat
hanging low among the reeds. The brilliant white web
consisted of a pouch and anchoring wings, all designed
with airborne grace and labyrinthine intricacy. I
photographed it and on my return home, sent it off to
my Adaptation collaborator, naturalist Laurie Smith,

giant sac spider — Miturga agelenina

who consulted a colleague at the WA Museum for identification. The following week I returned to the exact spot (about a kilometre along the lakeside track to the north of the thrombolite viewing platform at Lake Clifton) with Laurie, hoping to show him this little wonder, but it was no longer there. Wetlands are archives of the uncollectable: all I took away with me was an impression, that ephemeral anatomy of the invisible which we call memory.

In time I came to find this absorbing place full of questions and rewards.[9]

Very early on an April morning I joined a group that had gathered at the corner of Quail Track and White Hills Road, to collect tuart (*Eucalyptus gomphocephala*) fruit for the propagation program and ongoing research run by Murdoch University Senior Research Fellow, Katinka Ruthrof. There was already a bite to the dappled sunlight, and blindingly bright sky patches between the tuart branches. Underfoot, that characteristic summer's end crackle and dust of leaf litter. Looking up into the tuart canopies to find the tiny orbs of tuart fruit, it took time for my eyes to focus on the collage of contrasting shapes and shades. Each tree can simultaneously bear buds and almost-ripe fruits with open valves which had already broadcast their seeds. 'When the fruit falls, the valves gradually open, allowing the seeds to fall out. Strong winds, storms, can carry branches with fruit and seeds, scattering them far from the adult tree.'[10]

The weather forecast had been twenty-four degrees, cool enough (or so I thought) for the layers of clothing so necessary to protect me from ticks and their irritating bites. I had pushed a cotton scarf into the gap between my neck and the collar of my long-sleeved cotton overshirt, under that a T-shirt tucked into the waistband of my jeans, and pulled long socks up over the trouser legs. I wore gloves and applied liberal sprays of insect repellent under and over the clothes. But I was still bitten, though that discomfort came later and (as usual) the resulting sores lasted for weeks. Mostly,

you can't feel ticks as they bite you, it's only when the allergic itching begins and the welts are red and raised that you realise…

During the fruit-gathering there was a bright mood of camaraderie. We divided into groups of four or five, those of us new to this process gratefully falling in with the more experienced, and worked out an efficient division of labour: one hunter-gatherer wielded the long-poled tree-pruners, another developed the keenest eyes for a good harvest, and the rest of us happily worked together stripping the lower branches of gathered fruit, or pulling it off those that had been lopped from higher up.

I've a fondness for the idea that our ancestors worked this way, small tribal groups out in the open, each person finding her level of competence, giving guidance or accepting support from others. I like to fancy this pattern is in our genes and our memes, and that reconnecting with it soothes the soul – that wise old instrument which resists the hurried, individualistic beat of modern life. Because it soon seemed effortless, this free-flowing format, and we gathered thirty full calico bags.

That morning I learned more about the habits of tuarts than I might have at ten lectures. Katinka explained how the valves of tuart fruits also can open on hot days, or as the branches die as part of normal growth, and that although storm/wind and ants do help to spread the seeds, this will likely not result in tuart seedling recruitment. Recruitment of seedlings en masse occurs mostly following fire where seeds fall into ash beds, satiating ants and germinating. Occasionally seed falls from the adult tree and finds a safe site in a clearing.

But at Yalgorup National Park, the tuarts need all the help we can give them to regenerate, and following a brief rest for morning tea, Katinka took me into a tuart seedling restoration research trial, pointing out the meaning of different leaf colours at various stages of new growth and sharing the highlights of over a decade of experimental research.[11]

I marvelled at the particular qualities of these trees – which are so generous in the habitat they provide to other life forms, often at the cost of their own growth or even survival. Among the typical tuart dwellers, you'll find tuart bud-weevils, longhorn beetles, needle wasps, tuart leaf miners, female sawflies and their spitfire larvae, twisted moths and stick insects. In the trees' leaf litter live antlion nymphs and crab spiders. Mistletoe birds thrive on parasitic berries, brush-tailed phascogales — carnivorous, arboreal marsupials with acrobatic habits — and the vulnerable Western ringtail possums rely on this habitat, as do the black Carnaby's cockatoos, whose decline has been associated with tuart distress in recent years.

Three years later I would read further news of the trial's success: 'The first Tuart seeds to germinate in the Yalgorup National Park ash beds have been identified by Dr Katinka Ruthrof from Murdoch University. These tiny little seedlings will now spend the next 100 years growing into majestic Tuart Trees,

tuart bud-weevils — Haplonyx tibiali
   longhorn beetles — Phoracantha semipunctuata
needle wasps — Hymenoptera gasteruptidae
   tuart leaf miners — Nepticulidae sp.
female sawflies and their spitfire larvae — Pergidae
   twisted moths — Circopetes obtusata
antlion nymphs — Myrmeleontidae
bark crab spiders — Thomisidae stephanopis palliolata
   mistletoe birds — Dicaeum hirundinaceum
brush-tailed phascogales — Phascogale tapoatafa
Western ringtail possums — Pseudocheirus occidentalis

providing habitat for many threatened species. The created ash bed process supports the growth of Tuart seed and partners with direct seedling and planting of the project site. Thank you to all who contributed to making this part of our project a success'.[12]

Water provides a metaphor of space for people – of mental space, of freedom, free-floating. All water – river, sea, pond, lake – holds memory and the space to think. Water levels the spirit (spirit-level). It is the only opportunity we have in the landscape to see a truly level flatness.[13]

It's strange, given the sentiment with which western art evokes the four seasons, but at Yalgorup there isn't one particular time of year I favour over another, especially since I began to experience the life cycle there according to the six-season Noongar calendar which George Walley taught me. Bunuru, Djeran, Makuru, Djilba, Kambarang and Birak are so much more than melodic names; each one evokes Indigenous observations of the natural, accrued in this part of the world over millennia, and attunes all those who learn them to each season's wonders, its essential changes.

My friend Carolyn Marks and I went there in mid-Djeran (April and May), preparing for our collaborative installation 'Bush Journal'. The minute we walked beyond the tree line and reached the platform, a magnificent pair of adult black swans flew past, heading south, maintaining an arrow-straight trajectory low above the water. Characteristic white primary feathers in the wings highlighted their great spans. I regretted not having my camera ready, but undistracted by technology, fully appreciated the undulant grace and distinctive whoomp whoomp sound of their slow-motion wing-beats. And I remembered a story from a far culture, of swans that fly along the trail of sky-piercing song all the way to heaven, without dying.[14]

A profusion of claw marks in wet sand by the platform and a massed flock of grey teal ducks huddled on the dry thrombolite reef at water's edge to the south of us occupied me for a while. In the distance to the north were more teal, wading and feeding in rock pools. These were the largest groupings of birds I'd seen at Lake Clifton, and I wanted to photograph them, but smoke from a prescribed burn at Pinjarra was drifting over, imperceptibly at first, then the sky darkened and the smell of fire became alarming. Earlier in the year, the Noongar season Birak had been so dry and January's damaging bushfire was fresh in our memories. It had blackened acres of residential rural blocks and burnt homes in the nearby subdivision just across The Old Coast Road, on the boundary of the national park.

Carolyn used her mobile phone to check in with the local rangers and confirm that we were not in any danger. Reassured, I focused on the unusual visual effects the smoke created. Subtle gradations of colour and soft focus smudged the lake's fringing paperbark and peppermint trees, and the serrated horizon of tuart trees to the north-east looked like a watercolour wash. A calm surface, clusters of sculptural thrombolites and duck silhouettes reflected in rock pools completed a landscape where time so often seems to be suspended.

The lake is not always calm. As if to remind me of this, in the clear water beneath the viewing platform were more pieces of dislodged benthic matting, which I had first seen and photographed after a storm at the same time the previous year. I took more pictures of this latest damage to the lake bed, hoping to compare them. Fortunately, Carolyn quickly became immersed in the landscape, fascinated by all its aspects, sketching and taking notes. Our creative collaborations make for an intensity of shared observations and process, so she didn't mind my leisurely pace. It's a slowdown spell that works on me whenever I'm at the lake. We didn't even think about lunch until after two o'clock in the afternoon, and as usual, I still felt that was not nearly enough time. As we walked back from the platform, through

the lakeside trees, to our picnic spot, Carolyn asked me about the type of blue wrens I'd seen there on previous visits. As though on cue, a large family of splendid fairy-wrens landed around us, flitting from the ground to low branches, chattering as they searched out the tiny insects on which they feast. They seemed to be deliberately showing off to her, pivoting to catch the dappled light, so that it flashed on the male birds' blue tail and breast feathers, their courting plumage. These are companionable birds, and when they fly alongside me in the bush, singing melodiously or, quite often, garrulously, I feel as though I am being welcomed and watched over.

After lunch the smoke had lifted and that afternoon we explored the track which runs south between the rear of lakeside properties and the water's edge. Unlike the officially designated walking trail (leading north-west around the lake through dense thickets of peppermint and paperbark), the growth around this track seemed to have been cleared as parkland. Covered with soft, green new shoots and shady shrubs despite the long summer, the open vista was lush evidence of freshwater springs which seep from the ground along the lake's eastern shoreline.

Following the first Lake Clifton Festival nature walk, I'd been studying my guide to wildflowers of the South West for just such an occasion. Carolyn had an artist's interest in detail, wanting to name the sketches

she'd made that morning of <u>reed mace</u> and <u>bulrush,</u> <u>sea rush</u> and <u>pale rush</u>, <u>coast saw-sedge</u> and the aptly named <u>semaphore sedge</u> which dominate by the water. Flashes of crimson closer to the ground flag <u>samphires,</u> succulents which close-up look like popper beads of emeralds and rubies. Perhaps that's the reason samphire is also known by another name – glasswort. This first barrier zone around the lake provides water-filtering grasses and tasty food for the birds.

reed mace — *Typha domingensis*
bulrush — *Typha orientalis*
sea rush — *Juncus krausii*
108 *pale rush* — *J. pallidus*
coast saw-sedge — *Gahnia trifida*
semaphore sedge — *Mesomelaena tetragona*
samphires — *Tecticornia halocnemoides* and *T. indica*

Once on the southerly track we were 300–500 metres inland from the water's edge, in banksia and eucalypt woodland. Here an Edenic flourish of vegetation – honey myrtle, parrot bush, hibbertia – create an understory to the paperbark and peppermint trees. Naming the showy banksias is fun – *littoralis, menziesii, attenuate* and *grandis.* Towering above them are flooded gums and Yalgorup's iconic tuarts.

But it was two plants with which we were not familiar that fascinated us because of their distinctive fruit (reminding me that May in the Southern Hemisphere corresponds to autumn). However, you wouldn't want to eat these noxious weeds! Narrow-leaf cotton bush has spiky, elongated and pointed pods filled with white, downy threads. Apple of Sodom is a thorny, stout shrub bearing what looked like yellow and deep red (nearly black) cherry tomatoes. When we reached water again, I watched as a bird-shadow disturbed a school of small lake fish. As a singular, collective

honey myrtle – Melaleuca huegelii
    parrot bush – Banksia sessilis
hibbertia – H. racemosa, cuneiformis and hypericoides
    paperbark – mainly Melaleuca rhaphiophylla
            and cuticularis
peppermint trees – Agonis flexuosa
    flooded gums – Eucalyptus rudis

109

entity they swarmed, rolled and expanded, curled then contracted and changed direction, shape-shifting like liquid mercury. Swift and fluid as that ancient symbol for clear intellect and the flash of an idea, the shape of living fear is muscular, twists to the lithe choreography of survival instinct. Observing this and so much else in the animate world (the minute adjustments of birds in flight, for example), where thought seems inseparable from muscle, it is difficult to continue believing in the division of intellect and flesh, 'since our body is precisely our interface of exchange with the field of awareness...'[15]

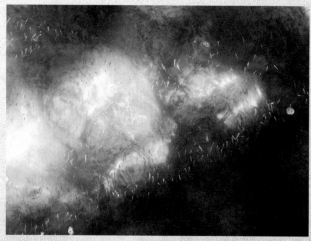

In the late afternoon, Carolyn and I visited Nancy and Galliano Fardin for tea and apricot slice. There we heard stories of recent wildlife encounters at their lakeside property: a plague of rabbits attracted raptors and foxes, who also took turtles; a neighbour's flock of sheep (perhaps deliberately unfenced to forage for feed during the seasons of Birak and Bunuru, the previous hard summer) that trod a corridor of tracks along the lake's fringing reed-beds, damaging soft ground, trampling eggs, nests and young turtles. And we talk of the remnant fish-trap in a lagoon which, through winter, shares a common surface with Lake Clifton. The fish-trap reminds us these waterbodies, which were once open to the Southern Ocean, provided the Bindjareb Noongar with a rich food source. And perhaps that's why, at times, I sense sadness and desolation at Yalgorup, where human and more-than-human life once abounded, sharing the edge.

My belief is that, despite increased scientific understandings, plants are inherently mysterious...I write in order to engage with this mystery.[16]

Nature writing, in both its experiential and research phases, and mostly in the creative process too, is foot-slog. It is about making contacts and getting permission to go places, and forming relationships with people who share your interest and, preferably, have had more experience. There's plenty of driving and weather and chance to contend with. The wild doesn't perform

on cue. Even if it did, that would be no substitute for the accretion of experience gained through repeated exposure to a place, its light, weather, inhabitants and particular features.

Then there is the thumbing through reference books, the searches online, the discipline of reference notes, and the fact that we live with change, so no research or nomenclature is ever the end of a story. The wonder lies in the details, and in the harmony of the whole. If a nature writer is a faithful witness to these, some grace and goodness will find its way into the work, because it is already there in the country around and within us. It is already 'created'. Language merely re-calls our awareness into its presence. But perhaps that is no mere thing, given our current, chronic and collective cultural amnesia about traditional connection to our natural habitats, an aversion to 'engaging the mystery'? Would I have missed it, were it not for the catalyst of a nature writing residency with SymbioticA?

Today, with Dick Rule and Bill Smart from BirdLife Australia, we have returned to the lakes in late Makuru (or mid-winter). South of Lake Pollard, almost where the southern shoreline curves around, Dick sets up his tripod and telescope. Bill has spotted a group of birds

wading at the waterline on the opposite side, directly across from us. A pair of hooded plovers, several grey plovers, red-necked stints and great knots – and also, quite distinct because of its larger size, a lone common greenshank. When the birds take to the air, I follow them with my binoculars down the length of the lake, and again later, as they fly south again after some time wading and feeding in shallows up at the northern end. The greenshank is always out in front of the flock, taking the lead with its long and characteristically coloured legs extended well beyond its tail.

Bill Smart beckons me over to what looks like large black ball bearings, clustered on a low mound of sand at the verge of the fringing vegetation. Rabbit dung, he exclaims. And if you wanted to catch a big buck, this is where you would wait for it to return. Not the females, though. Only the bucks.

It's important to be literate in the language of scats and tracks: they are animal signatures. During our

grey plover – Pluvialis squatarola
red-necked stint – Calidris ruficollis
great knot – Calidris tenuirostris
common greenshank – Tringa nebularia

113

walk along the shores, he and Dick frequently pause to ponder a set of paw prints in the sand, discussing the presence or absence of claw marks, explaining to me that feral cats and foxes have retractable claws, unlike dogs which do not. The European red fox (*Vulpes vulpes*) was deliberately introduced to Australia for recreational hunting in 1855 and fox populations became established in the wild in the early 1870s. They have a fondness for the plovers' eggs and have also decimated turtle populations, taking their hatchlings.

Before we leave the park, Dick Rule makes a short detour up a sandy track near the approach to Lake Pollard to show me a fine specimen of Fremantle mallee. The solitary eucalypt is growing in a clearing on the verge, so I can appreciate the graceful spread of its limbs. Later, on a map, he shows me where we have been. But even had I been looking at it as we bounced along the sandy corrugations, I'd never have followed our route. When you can't see into the distance and not even the sky is visible because tree branches meet overhead, when the track winds east, then west, then east again before plunging south, only an experienced guide could know where we are. The bush either side is beautifully gentle

114   *Fremantle mallee — Eucalyptus foecunda*

to look at: dappled light, feathery fronds and lavender-grey tree-trunks, yet from the vehicle, seems to have no distinguishing landmarks. It's fascinating how many senses we use to orient – the feel of ground underfoot, the direction of wind on skin, shadow movement, the polyphonic, stereo sounds of the bush. None of these are alert while inside a car and I think that we may be going around in circles, but decide that I am in safe hands.

While I am working all this out in my head, Dick and Bill are looking around for birds and keeping up a commentary honed to perfection during many years spent monitoring the near-threatened hooded plovers of this national park. They spot a black-faced cuckoo shrike, and describe to me, in detail, its distinct landing habit, which consists of ruffling and rearranging its feathers, together with a side-step motion, all of which helps with identification. A flock of yellow-rumped thornbills scatter from a roadside tree, showering tiny bodies like gold confetti. When we slow down to look

black-faced cuckoo shrike –
  Coracina novaehollandiae
yellow-rumped thornbill – Acanthiza chrysorrhoa

at the map, a grey fantail performs an aerial dance mid-track, right in front of the car, singing in a most conversational manner, its two-syllable 'chirp-chirp' alternating with longer pauses between a single chirp, like an inflection, deliberately shifting emphasis as in a poem or conversation. Both men describe this particular species' mid-air acrobatics and the way they build nests using spider webs to weave grasses into a pouch with a long tail, like a wine-glass stem. 'They are very sociable!' they concur.

And I could say the same about Dick and Bill and all the people who have shown me the treasures of these wetlands and shared, with me, this edge where they live and its mysteries.

grey fantail — Rhipidura albiscapa

1 Annie Dillard, 'Three', *The Writing Life*, HarperCollins, New York, 1990, p. 577.

2 Josephine Hart, *Damage*, (1991), Virago, London, 2011, p. 1.

3 George Eliot, *Daniel Deronda*, book 3, chapter 24, 1876.

4 Rebecca Solnit, <www.orionmagazine.org/index.php/place_where_you_live/>, viewed 8 July 2013.

5 Jiddu Krishnamurti (May 1895 – 17 February 1986) was an Indian speaker and writer on philosophical and spiritual subjects. There is no clue as to which of his teachings this line was extracted from; Roger McDonald attributes it to Krishnamurti in *The Tree in Changing Light*, Random House, Melbourne, 2001, p. 66.

6 Wallace Stevens (2 October 1879 – 2 August 1955) American poet and businessman. 'Notes toward a supreme fiction', Cummington Press, Nebraska, 1942. The quote is from the poem's first section 'It must be abstract', verse VII (opening line).

7 Jean Baudrillard (1999). 'Photographies.' as quoted by Dr Paul Thomas, founder and former director of The Biennale of Electronic Arts Perth in his thematic essay 'Stillness= contemplation and pattern recognition' for the BEAP 2007 Catalogue of STILLNESS The 3rd Biennale of Electronic Arts, Perth 10–23 September 2007, <http://blogs.unsw.edu.au/tiic/files/2011/11/BEAP_Stillness_2007.pdf>.

8 Terry Tempest Williams, *Finding Beauty in a Broken World*, Vintage, New York, 2008, p. 196.

9 George Seddon, *Sense of Place*, UWA Press, Perth, 1972, p. xiv.

10 Jan Ramage, *Tuart dwellers*, illustrated by Ellen Hickman, Department of Environment and Conservation WA, 2008, p. 28.

11 Dr Katinka Ruthrof, State Centre of Excellence for Climate Change, Woodland & Forest Health, Murdoch University, <http://www.treehealth.murdoch.edu.au/>.

12 Peel–Harvey Catchment Council, press release, 'We have germination Yalgorup National Park Ash Beds', 28 June 2013.

13 Roger Deakin, *Notes from Walnut Tree Farm*, Penguin, London 2009, p. 186.

14 Called *Yagatune* (the trail to heaven) in the language of the Dunne-za, traditional hunting people of Northeastern British Columbia in the forested Canadian subarctic; as studied by Canadian anthropologist Robin Ridington and described by Peter Knudtson and David Suzuki in *Wisdom of the Elders*, Allen & Unwin, Sydney, 1992, pp. 148–9.

15 David Abram, *Becoming Animal*, Pantheon, New York, 2010, p. 272.

16 John Ryan, botanical poet, *Two with Nature*, Fremantle Press, Fremantle, 2012, p. 9.

SONG OF THE LONG-NECKED TURTLE

You must gaze steadily at what is absent as if it were present by means of your mind.[1]

At the corner of my writing table there's the shell of an oblong turtle. An empty carapace, incised with geometric patterns, fixed above the plastron like a convex roof over an open-air stage. If touched, the shell rocks slightly on its underbelly armour, a lifeless movement that disconcerts me the way an unlatched shutter once did, swinging from rusted hinges as I passed an abandoned house on my way to school. This shell is a daily reminder that I've yet to see *Chelodina oblonga*, also known as a long-necked freshwater turtle, alive in its natural habitat.

The destruction of the species' natural habitat, many road kills of turtles searching for either a nesting site or a water body that does not dry out in summer, and natural predators are main causes of the Chelodina oblonga *population's decrease in numbers.*[2]

Turtle absence — a discernible blemish like the fall from grace — haunts me at the wetlands, where I am surrounded by wildlife. When I took up a writing residency based at Yalgorup National Park, I had been told these little creatures were endemic to that particular stretch of Australia's south-west coast. My interest was further piqued by an uncanny moment of human-to-turtle empathy that occurred as I was driving there for my first meeting with George Walley, who was to become my mentor in Indigenous culture.

My ensuing obsession with the turtles' disappearance is all the more surprising because of the aversion to a particular turtle that I developed forty years ago, while expecting my first child: after an autumn wedding we'd moved into our newly rented home on an old rural estate, where, in the spring, a very large and ancient land turtle emerged from its hibernation. I can still recall the clicking of its claws as it crossed the tiled terrace whenever I opened the kitchen door and how I shuddered at the sound of its shell scraping the shallow limestone steps, knowing it was lumbering down to the orange grove after me. That turtle stalked me through the veggie patch, back across the terrace and past the rose beds all the way to the clothes line. It was another species altogether, but before I went to Yalgorup, turtles were turtles. I had no interest in details. After my turtle 'stalker', I just wanted as much distance between us as possible. What changed?

Is it, as Gary Snyder wrote, that 'Awareness of emptiness brings forth the heart of compassion'[3]? Poets often speak of the heart. But does landscape have a soul, I wonder? Nature, that collective noun we are all part of, is one life, breathing and non-breathing, in which everything – even emptiness, it now seems to me – belongs. Each emptiness with its own specific shape and texture: the shell on my desk marked with the geometry of solitude, with a 'repose that divides being and non being'.[4]

The Department of Environment and Conservation (DEC) has attributed a recent spate of turtle deaths in suburban lakes to Perth's long, hot summer. Eight turtle deaths have been recorded at Woodlands' Jackadder Lake in the past five weeks.[5]

Just east of Fremantle, above the ridge where I live, storm clouds are swelling. It's Birak in the Noongar calendar, and January's heat has been oppressive for more than a week, but tomorrow, if the forecast is correct, the temperature will drop ten degrees to thirty-one degrees. A gravid oblong turtle won't lay her eggs when it is warmer than that. Her exodus from the safe edge-waters of the lake where she lives to the sandy dune where she must bury her clutch is often triggered by the barometric plunge which precedes a cool, wet change. Evolutionary survivors of Western Australia's long, hot summers, these turtles do not aestivate but are exquisitely sensitive to changes in atmospheric pressure.

In a 2012 radio interview with Margaret Throsby, Mark Tredinnick (whose illustrated book *Australia's Wild Weather*[6] had been published the previous year) observed that ninety-three per cent of our time is spent getting out of the weather. But, he observed, 'shifts of barometric pressure still do penetrate the closed, plastic or middle-class places we're in – and it affects us'.[7] I have noticed my own change of mood more than twenty-four hours before a storm and how often this happens when apparent weather conditions aren't suggesting a change. So the turtle and I have this in common, me in my brick-and-tile home, she in her 'marquetry of inlaid squares'. That image, from the poem 'To a box turtle' by John Updike,[8] wasn't inspired by the elusive *Chelodina oblonga* which is endemic to the south-west of Australia and an iconic feature of Pinjarra wetlands, the landscape of my poems and essays since 2009. But just now, I'll take anything I can get. I'm hungry for connections. Three years is a long time to wait for an encounter with a turtle in the wild.

Poems…are under way: they are making toward something.[9]

I had hoped my first turtle sighting would be serendipitous. Encounters which anyone might experience spontaneously while walking in wetlands are the focus of my writing. For that reason, I deliberately avoid visiting turtle sanctuaries and research sites, though I appreciate their role in conservation and education. Websites are another tantalising source of images and information, and often provide natural history's backdrop to traditional stories and beliefs. The oblong turtle is 'yaakan' to Bindjareb Noongar people; these creatures are culturally significant as totem and traditional food, their presence directly linked to creation times. Paintings and stories from the Pinjarra Massacre Memorial website record that these turtles have been embedded in an intricate system of taboos and food laws since the beginning of memory. And that was a very long time ago, as a book I was reading to my grandchildren reminded me: 'reptiles were the first vertebrates...to fully colonise the land surface. Their immediate ancestors, the amphibians, must periodically return to the water, or at least to a damp place to prevent dehydration and to lay their fragile eggs. Fossil records indicate that reptiles evolved from amphibians in the Permian period, some 300 million years ago. When reptiles left their amphibian ancestors behind in the swamp, there were no birds or mammals on land. These evolved from reptiles at a much later date'.[10]

After searching the fringes of every lake in the Yalgorup (where most have become too salty for this freshwater turtle), I tried likely haunts nearer my home – Blue Gum Lake, Piney Lakes, Manning Lake. Finally, I explored Mandurah's Goegrup Lake and the Murray River, where Pinjarra's 1834 Massacre took place and many Noongars whose totem was yaakan, were killed in such numbers by colonial soldiers that, deprived of their essential participation in the collection and distribution of this vital food, surviving Indigenous people were at risk of starvation.

I listened to this story, sitting in the shade of fragrant flooded gums on the banks of Bilya Maadjit (the Murray River's original Bindjareb Noongar name) as Noongar elder and artist Gloria Kearing told it to me and spoke of the relationship between human and non-human worlds. It is a relationship learned by each generation through the imprint of stories, customs and ceremonies in which sacred is not opposed to secular, as it has been framed by much Western thought.

At the start of every turtle hunt, adults and children acknowledge the non-human world with simple gestures – clapping their hands together, throwing sand into the lake. These actions signify a mutual interdependence: as nature's custodians, Indigenous people regard the turtle as a source of nourishment, to be approached with respect and gratitude. The preparation, cooking and consumption of turtle is prescribed by tradition. Turtle limbs are not cut before cooking; they must be torn from the body.

And certain portions of the animal are reserved, only to be eaten by the elders. In this way the dynamics of living and dying are experienced as a gift, willed by charismatic spirits.

Auntie Gloria, as she is respectfully known among Bindjareb people, has painted many river scenes but my favourite is one which depicts three turtles in the river and two more held by a female figure standing on the bank. She named it *Yarnup*, for the Indigenous woman of that name killed in the 1834 Massacre. I had seen the picture in an exhibition[11] long before I visited the river or met the artist, and found it poignant, strangely compelling. Years later, Kearing took me deeper into the memorial power of this bend in the river, an idyllic riparian landscape redolent with history and grief. This spirit of place infuses *Yarnup* and many paintings, such as *River of Spirits*, by Kearing and other contemporary Indigenous artists. To me, it felt like the memory of earth, and eventually I gave that title to a poem inspired by this immersive experience.[12] Most of my wandering has been around Yalgorup's wetlands, which are not directly connected to the river, though part of the same broader system of wetlands, waterways and creation myths. However, I felt drawn to learn more about the Murray's landscape and history. This seemed only natural to Kearing, who says local waterways and wetlands 'are all connected *in culture*, as are the creatures of the water, of the land and of the sky who depend on them, and humans present, past and future. I truly believe their spirits are still there'.[13]

She gave me permission to repeat her words, and I do so mindful of what my friend Glen Phillips has written: 'though I dare not appropriate the culture and legends of the Noongar people, I do care to know as much about the places of the Woggaal in their land and landscapes as I possibly can'.[14]

For my benefit, Kearing repeated some Noongar stories which have been handed on for thousands of years. These powerful teachings, she explained, discourage younger generations from damaging their environment or coming to harm themselves. In the past, the Indigenous people of Mandurah (which they called Mandjoogoordap, meaning 'place where hearts meet') depended on healthy river systems and water bodies for their wellbeing and survival. They learned conservation and interdependence at an early age. As Gloria's nephew George Walley recounts, little children were told that the fringing reeds of lakes like Lake Clifton, rivers and swamps 'are the Woggaal's whiskers, so you leave them alone'.[15] Treating this vital wetlands buffer zone with appropriate caution, they stayed clear of quicksands, leaving healthy vegetation to filter run-off and provide shelter for snakes, frogs and all the other creatures so vital to ecological balance and their own food supply.

Kearing remembered wading along the Murray River to the estuary with her mob as a child 'and being handed over my uncles' shoulders, piggy back, where it was deep'. This was in the warming months of Kambarang, when they began moving along the wetlands to the coast, enjoying the supply of yaakan or turtle, kooyar/kwiyar or frogs and gilgie or crayfish. It is how she learned the significance of waterways, at a time when her family still camped at the swamps[16] and lived off their abundant food. 'I was taught that there's a law for the fish, a law for the land creatures, a law for humans. And we each have to obey the law, then everything goes fine and there's enough for everyone.' As an example, she cited the prohibition on catching fish swimming upriver: 'We understood that they were going to spawn. Then later, when the fish swam downriver, they knew we could catch them. That it was right according to the law. *They knew* it was their last time, swimming the river'.

And that was how, as the Bindjareb people travelled

through country, moving camp according to the seasons and weather conditions, they individually and collectively embodied knowledge of our impact on nature: through first-hand, physical experience of the complex connections within ecosystems, and listening to the wisdom of elders.

I learnt a lesson about this approach to environment in my first conversation with Kearing, when I phoned her to say I was seeking stories specific to Lake Clifton, and immediately she broadened the conversation to include the estuary; Bilya Maadjit the Murray River; and lakes and swamps of Mandjoogoordap (Mandurah). To her it is all one country, experienced as having a living relationship to its human and non-human inhabitants. Many Noongar stories convey this inclusive web of wisdom in vivid imagery drawn from the immediate landscape. It is Bindjareb tradition that the female creation serpent, coming through and creating the estuary and all waterways linked to it, left her eggs at Lake Clifton.

Kearing told me many times that Lake Clifton has always been regarded as 'very special, very significant. Its thrombolites – known locally as Woggaal Noorook, which means eggs of the great female serpent – are not to be damaged or disturbed in any way. And the lake bed, which is alive, must not be broken'.

Cultural law includes strong warnings against disturbing the beds of any rivers or lakes. 'They are made by the great female Woggaal, it's where she went, part of her journey, making everything',

Gloria explained. 'Once, *everyone* knew that if they interfered with the river, pushed things into the lakebed, or dug them up, they or someone of their family could expect to fall ill.'

Our spirits are in the trees and the hills and the rocks and the animals. When you're born you come from the land and when you die your spirit goes back to the land. The spirit ancestors from the Dreaming gave us this law. This is our heritage. It doesn't change.[17]

It was George Walley who gave me the turtle shell which rests on my desk. Born in a small maternity hospital by the banks of the Murray River and now deeply versed in Bindjareb Noongar tradition, he teaches cultural history, plays the didgeridoo, writes and sings songs which communicate what he knows of country. The storyteller in me made a connection between George's music and the turtles' ancient voices, for yaakan have 'an impressive acoustic repertoire' (as the scientific description goes), though writing as a poet, I would say they sing.

130

I listened with particular attention when George told me where he had found the dead turtle because it was in 2009, driving to what I had hoped would be my first meeting with him, that I first became aware of the oblong turtles' plight, and it went like this: unfamiliar with the road to Mandurah – the freeway hadn't yet been completed – I took a wrong turn somewhere along the winding, 100 kilometre coastal drive from my house and began to head inland. Turtles can do the same thing when they are looking for a place to bury their eggs. Naturalist Laurie Smith[18] told me that their instinct is to clamber upwards (reverse geotaxis) away from water to dig the nest. On the other hand the instinct of neonates on hatching is to make their way downward to water (geotaxis). It seems that if the mother turtle overshoots the first rise on leaving water, she may become disorientated and end up several kilometres away. Unless rescued, she may perish, as could any hatchlings that emerge from her wayward nest, because they will not be able to navigate back to the lake.

In Western Australia, this very old landscape eroded only by vast time is being subjected to rapid change through relatively recent human activity.[19] Our transport routes are altering turtle terrain, with scant regard for the breeding trails which they have followed for aeons. Despite road signs on which the image of a turtle accompanies the warning CAREFUL – TURTLES CROSSING, many animals are crushed by vehicles. That day, while trying to navigate back onto the Mandurah road, I passed such a message and realised that I was

131

midway across a lake. A lake that had been sliced in two by the new road. It was Bunuru season, March, with no water around me, because many wetlands hereabouts are seasonal and dry out for half the year, so I hadn't noticed that the black swathe of tarmac actually cut through the summer lake bed's pale pink crust. At once, losing my way and arriving late didn't seem important compared to a turtle's tragedy. I imagined the mother turtle, burdened by a cargo of eggs, lumbering onto the hot surface as cars sped by. It was that seminal moment crossing the lake which awakened my sense of 'sharing the edge' with Mandurah's inhabitants, the ecologically rich landscape of Yalgorup National Park and its surrounding country.

The purpose of poetry is to remind us
how difficult it is to remain just one person
for our house is open, there are no keys in the doors,
and invisible guests come in and out at will.[20]

I had written of the wetlands as a place where I become 'a house without locks'[21] (and before reading

Milosz and Vallee's work) at a time when I was discovering that engagement with the natural world required me to make way for and admit unknown yet possible ways of being, to wayfare at the threshold between self and other. It was exhilarating and scary, this immersion in the ecotone where things meet; the margins where, as Jane Hirshfield describes with such passion in her book *Nine Gates*, transformations and transitions occur. In some blessed instances, differences become indistinguishable, and we are one rather than separate. As this inclusive paradox reveals, it is here that 'ecosystems are most rich and diverse – birds sing, and deer, fish and mosquitos emerge to feed at dawn and at dusk'.[22]

The empty turtle shell on my work table reminds me of an abandoned house which had seemed, when I was a child, inhabited by invisible forces and which swung its shutters open as I passed by. I associate that image with a creative state often referred to as flow – when the artist is intensely present and yet strangely absent. For an instant we become forgetful of self and pass through perception's permeable membrane; a veil lifts and, momentarily, we glimpse the whole. It is this entry into the world beyond ordinary states of consciousness, a transition which cannot be willed, that gives dancers and nature poets, musicians and painters the images, language and textures which imbue work with spirit. It strikes me as ironic that perspectives on nature arising from these experiences are often dismissed by scientists as 'magical thinking'. This seems an insuperable divide between Western gatekeepers of knowledge and Indigenous interpretations, perspectives and beliefs. A divide which I find non-existent, because it is these very insights which nuance nature writing and nest its wisdom. At the threshold of our deepest relationship with the non-human is what Hirshfield calls 'liminal wilderness' and 'a wilderness existence'.

My friends Nancy and Galliano Fardin, who for twenty-five years have lived on the eastern shore of Lake Clifton, understand the intimate nature of belonging to a particular place. Whenever I visit them, a kettle is always steaming on the wood stove in their kitchen. This is one of my favourite rooms anywhere. In it we are surrounded by natural textures and almost everything in sight has been hand crafted, even the whitewashed stone walls which the artist and his conservationist wife built together.

Galliano fashioned the kitchen cabinets from found wood; he made the table and chairs. The timber-slat staircase that scales the western wall to an upper storey reveals Galliano's minimalist elegance, his eye for function and design: each tread is centrally balanced on the single, supporting pole. On the particular visit I'm thinking of, the room was filled with straw-coloured sheaves of light, the mellow interior tinged by volatile oils of various local eucalypts, drifting in from the warm landscape. Uniquely shaped windows, designed and positioned to admit winter's late afternoon sunbeams at beautiful angles, framed sky which seemed clarified to salt's crystalline brightness. It was a time of year known to Noongars as Djilba. Puffs of white clouds drifted by, outlined in a fiery glow. This floating procession reminded me of a sheep flock I saw once in York, returning to the home paddock at sunset, gold halos edging wool on their backs.

Returning home is how I feel, visiting the Fardin family. Could that be what deepens the sensory impact of this place on me? That I identify with their sense of belonging, the intuitive intimacy and unforced continuity they enjoy with the ground underfoot and the marshes around them?[23] An aesthetics of authenticity characterises all our encounters here, whether we are walking across land where they have replanted the forest which once grew there, or sitting at the kitchen table, where talk flows to our adult children and back to the land, like tide along a familiar estuary. As old conversations continue, new stories begin, sharing the wild's flavour of immediacy, its vital unpredictability. I recognise the urgency and engagement which characterise local community or extended family news; it reminds me of the sense of country and clan which are so ineluctably twinned in the complex identity of islanders, for whom belonging to a place is felt as keenly as belonging to a bloodline.

I've missed that feeling for decades, but it has returned here, where country is the central character in all our conversations, our common relative. At the Fardin's table, it's mostly not weddings and graduations that are the focus of discussion (though they certainly get a mention), but how the land is recovering after a devasting bushfire, or what inappropriate new development is being proposed for the ecologically sensitive area, and whether they have seen any long-necked turtles. That is always my question, and on that winter's afternoon a couple of years ago Nancy replied, 'Not as many as there once were, but they are here'. Her tone was confident with hope and positivity. She's a member of FRAGYLE,[24] the group of concerned locals who monitor the wetland's wildlife. Nancy's words often sound to me like a fiat: they carry so much conviction, I almost believed she could will creatures into existence – or at least, survival. But

Nancy's a realist, who knows it takes action to prevent extinctions; that we are not creators, only curators and custodians. 'I thought the lake had become too salty for them?' I countered. It was then that Galliano, who sees more than the average person (and says less) spoke, quietly as though sharing a secret. 'There's fresh water at the shoreline, where the seeps are – *there* they are safe, covered by the reeds.'

Then they took me to see. We walked through the lake's innermost ring of paperbarks and sedges, to where a naturally formed pond – smaller and shallower than a household swimming pool – lay hidden deep in fringing vegetation. This is where they have often seen up to three turtles at a time basking on the sandy bed, under perhaps half a metre of water. Because it was August, when turtle hatchlings emerge, I asked Nancy if she had seen any signs yet that breeding was going well. 'Well now, we were lucky this year, though for a while we were *really* concerned', and then she told me how raptors were coming to the property in greater numbers, and she'd figured the birds had been attracted by Yalgorup's soaring rabbit population. Nancy knew they'd go for the baby turtles once they hatched, pick them all off before they reached the cover of water. She had just written a funding proposal, hoping for help to eradicate the rabbits, but of course that wouldn't have saved this year's babies. 'But, almost overnight, it seems a resurgence of calicivirus decimated the rabbits. With their food supply gone, the raptors and foxes moved away…' she said, and I shared her delight.

*A lake is the landscape's most beautiful and expressive feature.
It is earth's eye; looking into which the beholder measures the
depths of his own nature.*[25]

In this fragile coastal ecosystem, predicaments of
sharing the edge repeatedly take its inhabitants
to the cusp of life and death. In addition to this
geographic 'edginess', residents and conservationists
concerned for the wetlands' survival must constantly
counter attempts to develop surrounding real estate
for commercial purposes. Local groups have objected
to plans for a brewery, a caravan park and a quarry
at Lake Clifton, and as I write this piece, welcome
news arrives that an unpopular wind-farm proposal
has been withdrawn.

In a report to members by Hilary Wheater, chair
of FRAGYLE, I read that developer Ralph Sarich wrote
to the Chairman of the Lake Clifton Community
Group, which had opposed the wind farm, advising
them that: 'The family has considered comments and
general community concerns towards the proposed

project and has therefore decided to terminate the project in the interests of the local community...the greater community's views have been considered carefully and implemented'.

Wheater concluded her report by noting that 'Ralph Sarich and his family have to be congratulated on their consideration and deference to the locals, people who believed Lake Clifton would have been adversely affected by such a development'.[26]

There is no doubt that we need ways to generate sustainable forms of energy, but in a land as vast as Australia, it seemed transgressive to impose giant wind turbines on the slip of dunes and wetland that borders internationally listed Ramsar wetlands and a nationally protected, 'critically endangered' thrombolite reef.

There is a contradiction I heard about the Lake: it is a place of deep serenity that elicits very strong emotional responses by many people who go there.[27]

Viewed from my favourite vantage point – the viewing platform which straddles part of the thrombolite reef on Lake Clifton's eastern side – no buildings or powerlines interrupt this landscape. Across the water to the west, where a seacoast lies beyond sight over a scrub-darkened ridge, the far shore is a cuticle of salt-bright sand. Behind beach-fringing paperbarks, the dunes rise in a low, undulating arc. I need a wide-angled lens to capture their north-to-south curvature. The lake is twenty kilometres long. Only the dunes, silhouetted on the horizon like a small tsunami, divide azure sky from its mirrored waterface.

What brings me back here time and again is that this wetland – despite presenting a mosaic of earthy textures and smells – doesn't seem landbound at all, but a restless aquatic creature in quicksilver scales of light and shadow. I am enchanted by this. I never tire of watching the wind dimple the reflections of drowned clouds in this waded world of mutable surfaces. On the glowing screen of Lake Clifton, insects and waterbirds trace transient contour maps and meteorological charts in ever-widening circles, isobars and moving troughs that follow water's ephemeral geography. Sequential inversions, pooled between singing sand, alter my relationship to space. Tree canopies hang upside down on offshore shallows. Swans dip their long necks to graze on musk grasses. Sub-aquatic vegetation flourishes on every lakebed and at Clifton, at certain times of year and in particular conditions, attaches itself to the thrombolites. The thrombolites are peculiar structures growing underwater with glacial slowness. These rocks of deep time are a dramatic counterpoint to the unstillness of their surroundings, where coastal wind emphasises the transience of every wetland surface and mercurial light constantly alters the shape of sand dunes and shorelines, shimmering in sedges and tree canopies, whipping the lakes' surfaces to waves or wrinkling the soaks and rockpools. The thrombolites' presence is so powerful, however, that they draw me into *their* timescale, where I find respite from the rushing world which now comes right up to the eastern boundary of Yalgorup National Park.[28] For at least two thousand years, microbes have been forming a petrified landscape, known as the largest thrombolite reef in the southern hemisphere and revealed each summer when the lake's level drops. Summer or winter, the rocks seem to charge the immediate surroundings with dramatic tranquillity. It's a paradox which contributes to the metaphysical dimension of this place, which is impossible to ignore: intimations of it have surprised the most scientifically minded, widely travelled or most sceptical visitors I've accompanied there.

And yet I see their point, when scientists protest that there is no place for such 'sentiments' in their discipline. To me, the uncanny is suggested most fluently in poetry. A desire to express this indefinable quality has generated many poems. I've written of the water's edge at Lake Clifton as a place where the white-faced heron 'meditates / alone, still as the fossil mounds / pillowed round him, like a grey-robed monk / in his Zen garden of smooth, pale stones'.[29]

Of course, herons and turtles are creatures whose counterparts in mythic thought and traditional practices the world over symbolise the life–death–life cycle. In India the turtle is associated with a bodhisattva or Vishnu, in China it symbolises the north and the moon's phases, the Japanese pay it the same respect as they do the crane. From the hymns of ancient Greece to the 'rite hermetique' of eighteenth-century France, for Mayans, Dravidians, Sioux, Huron, Mongol and Dogon people, the turtle has been treated with respect. Stories and beliefs evolved which link it to generation, longevity, regeneration and notions of immortality. Snug between the domed and flat surfaces of its shell, the turtle became a mediator between heaven and earth. I was not surprised to learn that turtle plastrons were used by the ancient Chinese in a type of divination known as plastromancy.[30]

From imagination, which is so often the basis of empathetic relationships with the non-human, it's a small step to engagement. And engagement reveals a world of phenomena. An example of this is scientist Dr Jacqueline Giles's research. After learning in 2005

that the City of Melville in Western Australia was encouraging research into the long-necked turtle, then post-graduate student Jacqueline Giles still needed prompting from a mentor before choosing to study this species for her thesis. But her decision to focus on their vocalisations was taken in a moment, when a turtle which she was returning to the exact spot in Blue Gum Lake where she had lifted it out of the water began 'to roar like a dinosaur' in the bottom of her boat. When I interviewed her some years after this event, she told me 'I was more than intrigued. It was an absolute heart beat-skip moment'.

Like most of us, Giles had been unaware that turtles exhibit an extensive vocal repertoire. But she understood why they might, even though their recondite lives *imply* silence. Giles introduced her thesis abstract with this comment: 'These turtles often live in wetlands where visibility is restricted due to habitat complexity or light limitation caused by factors such as tannin staining or turbidity. For many aquatic animals, sound is a useful means of communication over distances beyond their visual acuity'.[31]

In the years that followed her first encounter with the ancient voice of this animal, she made recordings which revealed that long-necked turtles were intermittent callers, with an extensive underwater repertoire of seventeen vocal categories. These included squawks, hoots, cat whines, grunts, growls, drum rolling, wild howls, clicks, clacks, various chirps, cries and wails, and a sustained vocalisation, hypothesised to be an acoustic advertisement display.

Long-necked turtles have been around since Gondwanan times, not just as a genus, but as a species. But though they can be traced back to the age of dinosaurs, these cryptic creatures are disappearing. Out of sight and out of mind, there is a tragedy happening, unnoticed, until it will be too late. That's why it is so vital that we take time to understand and respect the world around us: for what we do not understand, we fear, and what we fear, we will hurt.[32]

Everything in the life of a poet is germinal.[33]

After meeting Dr Jacqueline Giles, I found myself thinking again of my friend the musician, poet and songman George Walley. For it seems he experiences little or no separation between scientific explanations and the creation stories his people have honoured for millennia. His world is both elemental *and* ensouled. As he sings of Yalgorup's prevailing wind, the south-westerly goolamwin,[34] it's as though he conjures its essence. This wind 'made our coastal ridges / cross-hatched sands / layered dunes',[35] I wrote after one of

144

my first visits. If it is the creating breath of this place, light is its running music. Together, wind and light are the architects of coastal plants. Wind and light inhabit the wetlands as a vast flock of birds might, as an animating presence, restless, lithe and unconfined.

Though the lake has moments of utter silence, it is never still. Light claims all surfaces, illuminating the landscape with organic patterns. Like a graphomaniac who has run out of paper, it inscribes the rocks, sand, samphire, sedge and trees. Under shallow water, the lakebed's rilled sand is webbed with filaments of gold. They form a dancing net that stretches from shore to the viewing platform, where it's transformed into strobes of bright and dark. Shadows and reflections cast by railings and timber boards stripe the rocks below in zebra patterns. Layered above them is a textured water surface, palettes of sequins and stars that shimmer and disappear as the sea breeze swings in.

George tells me that when he comes here, it's these bands of light he watches. I don't know if he is communing and, though it seems so to me, he doesn't attempt interpretations.[36] He attends. He pays deep attention.

Lyric cannot speak spirit – the ongoing of life, the sustenance of the spark – without being alive to violence.[37]

As I was writing this, news arrived online from Australian Geographic and Australian Associated Press[38]: at approximately 100 years old, Lonesome

George, the world's rarest tortoise, had died – putting an end to his species, *Geochelone nigra abingdoni*. He was the last Pinta Island tortoise at Galapagos National Park's breeding centre, on Santa Cruz Island. So the world is one species poorer. When I recall that reptiles evolved 300 million years ago during the Permian period, this extinction in our day points to a culture of loss, of absence and indifference as dramatic as it is tragic. For in losing our mythic imagination, we seem to have lost a sense of connection with life-forms other than our own. Our own *C. oblonga* have become best known as incidental roadkill, occasionally lamented in letters to the editor when the toll rises each breeding and hatching season. Most of us are likely to be reminded of turtles only after their death, and then only if we see the remains of that enduring shell. It's August now – hatching season again. I began this essay in laying season and I'm hoping, *still* hoping, that one day soon at the wetlands I'll come across a batch of tiny turtles at the water's edge, beginning their life. Hatchlings are the size of a twenty-cent piece, but carry within them an ancient lineage. So I'll be careful and tread lightly on that overlooked world.

146

Postscript: After I'd written this essay about my three-year search, and submitted it to the publisher as part of *The Lake's Apprentice*, I went to visit my friends at Lake Clifton, where I read it back to Nancy and Galliano. When I'd finished, Galliano said he thought we should try to look 'one last time' for turtles in their soak by the shore of the lake. How could I resist? We set off on the walk through paddocks and the lake's fringing trees, only stopping when we were standing shoulder-high in the barrier rushes around the soak. Then Nancy saw one! She shouted to Galliano that he should get it for me and without an instant's hesitation he plunged in, the legs of his long trousers soaking in the shallows. Soon I was holding a very alive, flailing turtle with my bare hands and its vitality felt as wondrous as that of a squirming, slippery newborn baby. Though this was unmistakeably *a turtle*, and I loved its earthy, swamp pungency, the gleaming green brown pattern of its shell. It had such robust limbs, and that inquisitive face at the end of a long neck, with its mouth nuzzling my thumb, created an instant bond. Though I knew I must, the child within me didn't want to return this perfect creature to the water, not just yet.

But of course I did. However, the immediate impact of those lived sensations have stayed with me – the turtle's unexpected weight, its dynamic movement and slipperiness, that muddy smell and the tremendous rush of holding its precious life in my hands.

SONG OF THE LONG-NECKED TURTLE

1   Parmenides, fifth-century philosopher. 'To the seeker after truth', as quoted by
    Anne Carson in chapter 4 of *Economy of the Unlost*, Princeton University Press,
    USA, 1999.

2   Jan Matiaska, 'Oblong turtle – *Chelodina oblonga*', viewed 17 July 2012, <www.
    carettochelys.com/chelodina/chelodina_oblonga_1.htm>.

3   Gary Snyder, quoted in Jane Hirshfield, *Nine Gates*, HarperCollins, New York,
    1997, p. 204, by Gary Snyder from *Mountains and Rivers Without End*. Reprinted
    by permission of Counterpoint.

4   Gaston Bachelard, *The Poetics of Space*, Beacon, Boston MA, 1994, p. 145.

5   Liam Croy, 'Long, hot summer to blame for turtle deaths', *Stirling Times*, 15 March 2011.

6   Mark Tredinnick, *Australia's Wild Weather*, National Library of Australia, Canberra, 2011.

7   *Midday with Margaret Throsby*, 1 February 2012, radio program, ABC, Sydney.

8   John Updike, *Collected Poems 1953–1993*, Alfred A. Knopf, New York, 1993, pp. 226–27.

9   Paul Celan, quoted by Edward Hirsch, 'Heartland', Poetry Foundation,
    2011, viewed 27 June 2012, <http://www.poetryfoundation.org/learning/
    article/177205>, Paul Celan said: 'A poem, as a manifestation of language and
    thus essentially dialogue, can be a message in a bottle, sent out in the – not
    always greatly hopeful – belief that somewhere and sometime it could wash up
    on land, on heartland perhaps. Poems in this sense, too, are under way: they are
    making toward something'.

10 Steve Parish, *Amazing Facts: reptiles*, Steve Parish Publishing, Oxley, Qld., 1997, p. 4.

11 *Art On The Move, Pinjarra Massacre Memorial Exhibition*, Fremantle Prison,
    Western Australia, 5 February – 14 March 2010, viewed 20 October 2010, < www.
    artonthemove.com.au/content/Exhibitions/Pinjarra+Massacre+Memorial/>.

12 'The memory of earth', awarded the Tom Collins Poetry Prize 2010, *Westerly*, vol.
    56, no. 1, 2011, pp. 96–7.

13 Personal interview with Gloria Kearing, Pinjarra, 4 March 2012 for my essay in the
    Adaptation exhibition 2012 catalogue.

14 Glen Phillips, 'The elusive serpent: snakes and dragons as a symbolic presence
    in Australian literature', paper presented to *The Thirteenth Biannual Conference
    of the Australia-China Studies Association*, Xihua University, Chengdu Sichuan
    Province, China, 5–8 July 2012.

15 *Barragup Yarns*, Indigenous history film project, Mandurah WA, 2012.

16 Until the early 1970s, Indigenous people were not allowed into Mandurah town after dark and so many Bindjareb Noongars continued to live traditionally on the land. Franklyn Walley, *Barragup Yarns: an Indigenous history film project*, Mandurah, WA, 2012.

17 Ralph Winmar, 'Walwalinj: The hill that cries' (Manning, 1996), cited by Department of Education and Training 2008, viewed 10 September 2012, <http://www.det. wa.edu.au/aboriginaleducation/apac/detcms/aboriginal-education/apac/regions/ beechboro/history-of-the-swan-district.en?oid=MultiPartArticle-id-9430685>.

18 Laurie Smith was my early collaborator on 'Sharing the edge', an eco-art project at SymbioticA, University of Western Australia, where I was writer-in-residence.

19 Victoria Laurie, *Australian Geographic*, no. 109, 2012.

20 Jane Hirschfield, Czeslaw Milosz, 'Ars poetica', translated by Lillian Vallee, quoted by Jane Hirchfield in *Nine Gates*, HarperCollins, New York , 1997, p. 205.

21 Annamaria Weldon, 'My lover, the sea', Sea Things project, The Red Room Company 2012, viewed 1 December 2010, < http://redroomcompany.org/poet/ annamaria-weldon/>.

22 Jane Hirschfield 'Writing and the threshold life', *Nine Gates*, HarperCollins, New York, 1997, p. 213.

23 Yalgorup is Bindjareb Noongar for 'place of swamps'.

24 Friends of Ramsar Action Group for the Yalgorup Lakes Environment.

25 Walter Thoreau, *Walden*, quoted in Gaston Bachelard, *The Poetics of Space*, Beacon, Boston MA, 1994, p. 210.

26 Hilary Wheater, 'July 2012 Report to Members', Friends of Ramsar Action Group for the Yalgorup Lakes Environment.

27 Cecelia Cmielewski, manager SymbioticA, catalogue, *Adaptation exhibition* 2012, p. 7.

28 The Perth to Bunbury Highway was opened 20 September 2009.

29 Annamaria Weldon, 'Heron on the rocks', *Creatrix* no. 9, Perth, 2010; p. 182 of this book.

30 Jean Chevalier & Alain Gheerbrant, translated by John Buchanan-Brown, *The Penguin Dictionary of Symbols*, Penguin, London, 1996.

31 Jacqueline Giles, 'The Underwater Acoustic Repertoire of the Long-necked, Freshwater Turtle *Chelodina oblonga*' abstract for Ph.D. thesis, School of Environmental Science, Murdoch University, Perth, Western Australia, September 2005.

32 Dr Jacqueline Giles, interview with author, Mundaring, 4 August 2012.

33 Gaston Bachelard, *The Poetics of Space*, Beacon, Boston MA, 1994, p. 70.

34 Noongar word for wind that blows off the Indian Ocean.

35 Annamaria Weldon, 'Even the Wind', *Landscapes: the Journal of the International Centre for Landscape and Language*, vol. 3, no. 2, 2009, article 36, available at <http://ro.ecu.edu.au/landscapes/vol3/iss2/36>.

36 George Walley, conversation with author, Lake Clifton, 14 April 2011.

37 Sophie Mayer, 'De-inventing the wheel: circles within circles in John Kinsella's 'Armour', viewed 1 July 2012, <http://www.wolfmagazine.co.uk/26review.php>.

38 *Australian Geographic*, 'Galapagos tortoise Lonesome George dies', Newsletter, 25 June 2012, viewed 26 June 2012, <http://www.australiangeographic.com. au/journal/lonesome-george-galapagos-dies.htm>.

NATURE NOTES
the opposite shore

*The seashore environment is a harsh one. The low fertility of the
sand, its reduced humus content, poor water-holding capacity
and above all its instability and the salt-spray factor prevent many
species of the native flora from becoming established there.*[1]

My first visit to the far side of Lake Clifton coincides
with the day particles of a Chilean mountain float
above Western Australia, though I don't realise at the
time that it is volcanic ash shrouding the sun. A sooty
yellow haze over the wetlands makes it harder than
usual to see where salt-marshes end or lakes begin,
impossible to find the saturate edges where sand-flats
bleed to sky. No doubt Yalgorup's water, land and
horizon either know their own borders, or don't
care to. Here, only I insist on defining, outlining
and separating. But down the years this elemental
place, which has taken millennia to make its living
waterstones, will reshape my thinking. There is
country which can change our minds.

Few people get west of Lake Clifton unless they
are on conservation business. Without special permits
and transport, the westerly shore directly opposite the
thrombolite viewing platform seems inaccessible. Private
property and protected national parkland skirt the lakes.
In the three years it has taken me to meet my guides
to that far side, it has acquired a mystique reserved for
the unknown and unattainable. I have gazed west at it,
across the water from the thrombolite viewing platform,

and peered through binoculars. So when I set out with BirdLife's Dick Rule and Bill Smart, who have once more volunteered to take me on their scheduled count of *Thinornis rubricollis,* the vulnerable hooded plovers which often breed at the Yalgorup lakes, I don't ask questions about our destination, and try not to get my hopes up. I realise we are heading for the seaward shores of the Yalgorup's most northern lakes when we reach the Sarich property, and Bill Smart jumps out to retrieve a key left for us by arrangement. He says it will open a series of gates. As Dick drives through the first one, I feel a rush of excitement and longing. It reminds me of my childhood, of how I loved to find the phrase 'beyond limit of maps' in a book…

Like a dramatist's pathetic fallacy, strange weather conditions conspire with my love of mystery and adventure.

What is the pattern which connects all the living creatures?[2]

Beyond Yalgorup's limestone ridges and swales is a wild coastline where the Southern Ocean salts the breeze. This is the wetlands' silver-blue edge, wide open to weather. It holds nothing fast, not the moment nor its shape-shifting lakes; not the sand streaming from dune blow-outs like lions' manes, nor the migratory flocks which eventually return to their Arctic tundra, flying away by night as though they cannot bear to see the refuge they are leaving. Only the water-stones seem permanent here, thrombolites which have been

154

growing two thousand years. We are losing them, too. Adrift in this immense transience, I look for the reassurance of structure, and find patterns everywhere. Feathers, scales, birds in flight, tree bark; shorebirds' claw marks like script in dried mud, fractal patterns in cracked and drying shorelines, ripples of water weaving light to a golden mesh on the shallow lakebed. Patterns which imply, and then insist upon, a whole beyond individual life forms.

It takes – it took me – time to attune, in Australia, to nature's microscopic patterns in the macro. To European eyes, the bush can seem chaotic, untameable, without logic. It is the intricacies of Australian flora, their architectural response to adaptation in conditions which challenge survival – from the tiny *Drosera*, a carnivorous sundew flower, clinging for life on a granite outcrop, to the candle-shaped bull banksia flower and its seed pod – which continue to amaze me.

Everywhere, growth reaches and radiates, branches or worms through the elements, streaming in water, riding on air, burrowing into earth. This movement is nature unfurled, the choreography that sustains hive and anthill, which guides flocks of birds coming in to roost, and those leaving on their restless migrations. Growth is the insistence on life that safe-keeps the temporarily homeless who abide on the wind: swarming insects, drifting pollen, suspended sands. Resilience is embedded in the adaptable benthic microbes, which I have seen under a microscope, that build anchorite cells around themselves, and in weather patterns which create shorelines from wave-wash and storm berm,

piling crushed shells and windswept sand into ridges. Botany distils the logic of adaptation.

A Guide to the Coastal Flora of South-Western Australia[3] describes the roles played by dune plants, according to their different habitats. Knotted club-rush, marram grass and coast sword-sedge, for example, are rhizomatous plants with laterally spreading foliage that stabilises large areas of coast and has the ability to survive burial due to the rapid vertical growth of leafy shoots. The prostrate mat plants, typically *Tetragonia decumbens* (sea spinach), *Carpobrotus aequilaterus* (pig-face) and *Cakile maritima* (sea rocket) protect areas from erosion. This is only a fraction of the species found on mobile dunes, half of which have succulent foliage, and some plant foliage is shaped to act as a trap for drifting sand.

At each visit I have observed how, from the light-seeking stems and barrier-shaped leaves of dune plants that stabilise the coast with hair-mesh roots, to the great trellises of branches in the sky and their duplicate

knotted club-rush — *Ficinia nodosa*
marram grass — *Ammophila arenaria*
coast sword-sedge — *Lepidosperma gladiatum*

mass knotting below ground, the pattern builds cell by cell. How every living thing strings itself into the weaving: a spider leaves the edge to swing through air spinning the day's first silken line, seeking a distant place to hitch it. Hanging by a thread, its life is given to the momentum of this creative arc. Confident of anchorage, claiming space to survive, the spider spreads a web. The fundamental pattern of creation is radiant – from wind-braided reeds, book-leafed paperbarks and funnelled ant-hills to stacked clouds and ripples in sand-dunes, which make wind visible. Perhaps

this is one reason why, no matter how chaotic my thoughts and emotions, immersion in nature clears my mind. The purposeful life of an ecosystem is a palpable presence: even if evidenced only in the fallen feather of a bird, whose trajectory has already taken it beyond the horizon, Yalgorup connects me to a higher order. That order does not reflect fixity. It reveals dynamic ripples emanating from the edge, the visible imprints of an unseen, creative core.

It is obvious the answer's found all around in what endures, and knows enough to go on being – acting as if we weren't here.[4]

I am comforted by my woollen cap and gloves. Today the winter sun is a hazed circle behind pale, tissued cloud. With no traffic or industry for miles around, I can smell faint volatiles of eucalypt mingled with the salty ozone gusts off the lakes. We are looking out for early blossoming cockies tongue, which flowers here from late Djeran, Makuru, Djilba and Kambarang, until early Birak – those Noongar seasons between May and December. No wonder it's Mandurah's emblem. But we are too early and despite walking at five lakes, we find only one specimen. First of the season, its pod-like coral petals are a welcome flash of warm colour on this overcast day.

We pass on foot through an area west of Duck Pond which still looks disturbed – flat patches of ground, uncharacteristically bare of any growth. Dick Rule points it out as the location of a camp site during the time of the 10th Light Horse.[5] 'There's remnants of fencing around here where they tethered the horses', he adds, gesturing at the overgrown bush beyond. We are somewhere along the Bridle Trail from Island Point (on the west side of Harvey Estuary) to the southern terminus (at Wellesley Road just east of Binningup). Most markers for this trail have disappeared and the water holes need signage as well. Waroona, Peel and Mandurah produced a map in 1999 but since then the Forrest Highway freeway extension has blocked access for horse riders to the full stretch of the trail.

Rounding a bend in the track we find the skeleton of a full-grown, long dead kangaroo lying undisturbed on the ground. The bones have been picked clean and are bleached white, in dramatic contrast to their emerald bed of flattened sedge. This narrow trail to the beach is barely wider than the animal's pelvis, so we have to step carefully around the remains. I notice I'm feeling a profound and natural peace around this orderly arrangement of bones and their sculptural precision.

A few more steps and we reach Duck Pond. On the far shore is a brilliant display of samphire which has turned ruby and glows against a foreground of ashen sand and the fringing trees' dark foliage. Silvered skies and water surfaces on this monochrome day intensify colour's impact, which is like a shout ringing out on a deserted mountainside.

We take great care walking along the lake shoreline because hooded plovers' nests are easily crushed, and so well camouflaged by natural colour blending and

samphire — Tecticornia halocnemoides and T. indica

161

their low profile that one could be stepped on quite easily. The breeding birds make a scrape in sand above the high water mark (usually, but if they get it wrong due to wind or storm, the nest is doomed). Sometimes the scrape is lined with seashells. The male and female plovers take turns sitting on the eggs, but if they move away to feed or to try to protect the site, the eggs are left unprotected from the elements, especially fierce summer heat — and vulnerable to animal predators like the <u>red fox</u>, snakes (among them the <u>dugite</u>), and <u>silver gulls</u>. And then there's human carelessness, such

red fox — Vulpes vulpes
dugite — Pseudonaja affinis
silver gull — Chroicocephalus novaehollandiae

as trail-bike riders and four-wheel drivers joy-riding along the beach. Even on foot, park visitors may do irreparable damage to the nests and hatchlings by taking dogs into the protected areas, especially if the dogs are unleashed, as this stresses the birds (who recognise dogs as their natural predators). I can't understand it. These shores seem to me places where one would naturally want to tread lightly.

Except for tyre-track scars, which linger on the otherwise undisturbed shorelines, the few metres of wide open ground between water and tree line are characterised by pristine, pale, tightly packed sand with delicate outcrops of limestone and showy clumps of sedge and samphire. These are the plants of a naturally occurring water-garden; their forms and colours, the patterns of their distribution, unmediated by human hands, their design the outcome of adaptation and evolution. And while we read in them the natural history of a place, its living record, they are just being

themselves. For too many of us, walking in such remote, wild places is an almost forgotten sensation. It feels instinctual to step softly here, as though my body recalls other meetings, remembers other places where I have never been.

Water oozes from the sand underfoot. We have reached damper ground. Bill reminds me that groundwater springs drain into the lakes, as rainwater collects over time from the higher limestone ridges (which run like ribs under the dunes, parallel to the coast), seeps and percolates to the lowest ground, feeding Yalgorup's contained system of interdunal lakes. I stop and, crouching to touch the sand where it's soaked, marvel at this 'tear duct of the earth', a phrase from Roger Deakin's *Notes from Walnut Tree Farm*.[6]

He could tell a bird by a mark, a piped note, an attitude in the air. When I marvelled at this, he said identifying a bird was similar to making a poem or a finished piece of work from the kind of notes I stopped to make in my book, crouched down out of the wind.[7]

Below Boundary Lake, heading south, and adjacent to Lake Clifton's westward shore, lies Linda's Lagoon.

Previously known as Teal Lake, it was renamed after the Western Australian scientist and pioneer researcher into thrombolites, the late Dr Linda Susan Moore (1956–2010).

A colleague of Dick Rule, from BirdLife, is not with us today but has told Bill and Dick of a recent sighting of a hooded plover's nest near here. By the time we reach the location at Swan Pond, I am well and truly ready to appreciate the good fortune of this lead. We have walked around the shoreline of many lakes already – Duck Pond, Boundary Lake and Linda's Lagoon – searching for, but not sighting any nests and only spotting a few birds. I've photographed several hooded plovers, struck by the clarity of their dramatic, elegant markings, their habit of moving around in pairs and strong site fidelity. Even before I learn of the tricks they play to fob off predators, I realise these birds have personality! I am thinking how oddly charismatic they are when suddenly the nest is simply there, at our feet.

It looks perfect. Like an image from some Australian Geographic documentary, or BirdLife journal (and I reference them deliberately, those contexts in which I am most accustomed to 'discovering' wild nature). To encounter such rare treasure in its wild surroundings feels so exciting and much more dramatic than seeing a photograph or documentary. I ponder why this is so and realise that being there in the flesh myself, just another body in the landscape, all my senses are alert to how vulnerable life is. Or as David Abrams phrases it: 'our animal senses, co-evolved with the animate landscape, are still tuned to the many-voiced earth'.[8]

Hooded plover's eggs are strikingly beautiful: that perfect ovoid form, a smooth surface which can be the colour of damp sand or tinged to the exact green shade of its surrounding terrain, covered with dark speckles that look like flecks of dry kelp. In this scrape the eggs are sand-coloured and seem filled by light. The 'nest' has been lined with broken white bivalve shells and the empty, coral-coloured *Coxiella striatula* cone-shaped shells left after the birds feed: such deliberate preparation, I think, poignant evidence of many purposeful journeys. There's delicate intricacy (like a jeweller's setting for

precious stones) in the encircling low-relief limestone and samphire, a placement birds choose for the scant protection or camouflage it provides for these eggs which rest on the ground.

Love what the place in the moment expresses, and let it go. The shore may teach you this. The birds come and go and come and go. The waves are never absent and they never stay.[9]

Light is a preoccupation of painters, poets and photographers. Many of my favourite writers allude to the particular quality of winter light on and around open water. Their words don't need embellishment, because all of us have witnessed this phenomenon. And though it is never twice the same, even in the same location, there is a recognisable palette of monochromatic subtleties and elemental affinities. 'Wind-light streams from Holy Island', wrote the poet Ian Burgham, of the Orkneys, in

his collection *The Stone Skippers*.[10] Along the river, he saw
linen-white light. On the morning of the Winter Solstice
in Fife, Kathleen Jamie called it 'a weakling light'.[11] And
writing about Orford Ness, in his book *Notes from Walnut
Tree Farm*, Roger Deakin noted 'the grey light, where the
shingle desert ends and the sea begins'.[12]

Occasionally, the three of us out here today
counting hooded plovers – Dick Rule, Bill Smart and
I, all members of BirdLife Australia – wonder whether
smoke from a scheduled burn-off in the distant hills
is causing the dim, diffused light. But distracted by
its shadow-free effects on my photographs, my focus
is directed at getting the best shots of this landscape

around me. It is only many hours later, listening to the radio news on the 100 km drive home, that I learn a cloud of volcanic ash settled over Perth earlier in the day. Blown halfway around the planet from South America's erupting Puyehue volcano in Chile, it was dense enough to halt all incoming and outgoing flights from Western Australia's international and domestic airports.

The explanations for changes in light are rarely so dramatic. In this Southern Hemisphere wetland on the coast of Western Australia, there are many shadowless winter days when a high grey sun is shrouded by overcast sky. On such days the marsh light seems to come from outside time itself, as though it had been exhausted and paled by the aeons, as though it were a fossil leached of colour, as though it were the world's first light, a primitive light, still falling and perpetually innocent of stain.

Far from offering an untrustworthy account of things, our senses disclose an ever-shifting reality that is not amenable to any finished account, an enigmatic and encompassing field of relationships to which we can only apprentice ourselves.[13]

Timelessness is on my mind: for the past three years, I have looked across Lake Clifton from the viewing platform above the thrombolites, at the lake's eastern shallows, and wondered what the far shore was like. I've gazed at its pale sand strands and the characteristic dark outline of fringing trees. But even through

binoculars, at a distance of a kilometre or perhaps more, I could not distinguish individual features. Over time, as my curiosity grew, I began to think of it as an unreachable shore, until it acquired a kind of fabled quality. That morning's diffused light added an uncanny, monochromatic effect to the scene as I finally walked onto Lake Clifton's western edge.

Across the water, absurdly shrunk in the new perspective, is Lake Clifton's viewing platform, always an important feature of my past visits to the thrombolites. Its curved design extends out to deep

water, dominating the most accessible portion of the eastern foreshore. I've walked it countless times and sat on its boards on a late summer morning, in the balmy air of Bunuru, dangling my legs over the water, a flock of over thirty welcome swallows and tree martins perched peaceably on the railings around me. I've photographed rising and falling water levels through the seasons from this vantage point, watched the white-faced heron feed not metres away, grey teal ducks huddled together on the shoreline and black swans fly past me level with my shoulders. In spring and in autumn, I have watched the full moon rise from behind the peppermints, paperbarks and tuarts of the national park, and seen its reflection float among the pale mounds in the lake. So now, it is a shock to look across from the opposite side, barely making out the structure – and when I do, to see it dwarfed by the great twenty-kilometre length of lake – an expanse that seems more visible from where I am standing this

time. Looking back at the platform in this way, I feel
I have moved on and sense I am growing beyond my
fascination with the living fossils, that I am going to
explore more of Yalgorup. But I know, too, in some
deep sense that I will always be the lake's apprentice.

1   'Dune plants and their environment', *A Guide to the Coastal Flora of South-Western Australia*, handbook no. 10, WA Naturalists Club, Perth, 1973, p. 25.

2   Gregory Bateson, 'Introduction' (originally delivered as a lecture at the Cathedral of Saint John the Divine in New York 17 November 1977), *Mind and Nature – a necessary unity*, Bantam, Toronto, 1980, p. 9.

3   Handbook no. 10 published by WA Naturalists Club, Perth 1973, pp. 25–43.

4   Ian Burgham 'The one true cross', *The Stone Skippers*, MacLean Dubois, Edinburgh, 2007, p. 24.

5   See history of 10th Light Horse, World War 1, viewed 19 June 2011, <www.peeltrails.com.au/trails/view/5/16/10th_Light_Horse_Bridle_Trail>.

6   Roger Deakin, *Notes from Walnut Tree Farm*, Penguin, London, 2009, p. 68.

7   Kathleen Jamie, *Findings*, Sort Of Books, London, 2005, p. 54.

8   David Abram, *Becoming Animal*, Pantheon, New York, 2010, p. 264.

9   Mark Tredinnick, *The Land's Wild Music*, Trinity University Press, San Antonio, Texas, 2005, p. 132.

10 Ian Burgham, 'What's to become of us', *The Stone Skippers*, McLean Dubois, Edinburgh, 2007, p. 60.

11 Jamie, *Findings*, op. cit, 'Darkness and Light', p. 1.

12 Deakin, *Notes*, op. cit., p. 221.

13 Abram, *Becoming*, op. cit., p. 307.

PART II

*The Lake's apprentice
and other poems*

CONTENTS

THE LAKE'S APPRENTICE

Midwinter my lake is clouds
adrift on a glossed photograph,
archipelagos of sacred stones
drowned in archival sky, ripples
shaping fossil mounds to rune-bones.

By midsummer my lake is a sculpture
park lapped by sun, receding
water, bleached shores of thirsting
microbes that survive by sipping
groundseeps (and I breathe in, we
are breathing oxygen they release).

Millenia ago these thrombolites
        – the Woggaal's eggs –
painted ozone blue sky
from knot-worked stone.
Now they are turning me
into the lake's apprentice.

Their practice of creation
takes elements and memory
then grows, but never
leaves this landscape.

Slowed to a benthic pace,
discovering time not
as life's enemy but its keepsake,
patiently changing forms
(winged, scaled, clotted), I am
finding adaptation is my nature.

HERON ON THE ROCKS

At lake's edge, low on the ground
the white-faced heron meditates
alone,
      still as the fossil mounds
pillowed round him, like a grey-robed monk

in his Zen garden of smooth, pale stones.
This is the way a hunter spells patience,
waits
      on his own at the threshold of life
and death, hinged limbs folded artfully

out of sight. Only his eyes glint.
He is following the rock pool's shrimp,
darting
      fish. Marking their depth,
keeping his power coiled, deaf

to the hungry cries of stilts and grebes
until in one lunge water, scales and flesh
cleaved,
      he raises the kill like a trophy
as he retracts his neck, opens his bill

to flip the fish and with a swift gulp
that long and peristaltic throat
swallows.
   He quivers, then, with ritual
elegance the skilled assassin tucks away

his javelin between soft breast-feathers
and like an origami crane at rest
folds
   himself down, becomes
a vague shadow at lake's edge again.

WOGGAAL NOOROOK

In the beginning, her eggs
a clutch of living stones, earth's
immersed lungs, windows
of a dream,
open.

If they spoke
       just once…
we would hear the first breath
before it became everything
before it became Yalgorup.

THE MEMORY OF EARTH

We cannot list the victims' names, we cannot call it a Massacre Site or even a Significant Aboriginal Site, the site is only allowed to be known as a Battle Site.

I

The wetlands have watermarked her. Rivers
fill her pen. Pinjarra's lakes and creeks won't
stay asleep in their own beds. Her pages
are soaked with run-off. She is an inlet
where tides rise and fall, a blue eye drifted
by clouds. The wild goes walkabout through her
notebooks, scattering grain and spores along
the margins. She hears trees shed bark, seed skins
crack and split,   tails slithering through sedges.

Fox and heron make her rooms thoroughfares.
Claws scrape dry sand, paws scuffle leaf litter.
She tracks small prints that vanish at the edge
of soft and damp where savoury marsh samphire
is spreading   into the corners of poems.

2

In the morning now she wakes with the scent
of river gums in her sheets. The ink stains
on her pillows are rimmed with salt. Through her
Bilya Maadjit flows transparent as rain,
cold and clear as the first day she entered
it, turning her fluvial, insistent
as blood but deeper than veins, inscribing
her ochre   mapping the history of pain.

Under eucalypt branches, the white threads
of stamen stitch tannin water, but this
Kambarang sunlight is leaded with shades
and a silence like sleep leans on the green
terrace where mia mias clustered, before
the morning   that those musket shots shattered.

3

She is earth from earth, feels the truth buried
here. Holds her pen like a spade, to disturb
the surface, shovels until nib hits bone
and ground cries out   this was a massacre.

Flooded gums have forested the red dirt
on her desk. Their roots, webbed over its edge
and anchored in air, hang in tangled skeins
the way that hair comes loose when women weep
hiding their eyes, covering the babies
that cling to them as they crouch in hollows
beneath the Murray's banks   where she sees them
in watery reflections of trees, their
footholds eroded by time and grief, yet
still alive   in the memory of earth.

BIRTHBED

At sundown we reached the lake,
its surface ablaze out west
the near shore in shadow
       where a salt-marsh loomed,
       calm old midwife waiting
       for full moon to rise.

Under the water, thrombolites
were discs of light, acres
of cratered stone shaped
       like cocoons, memories
       the wintering lake held
       deep in amniotic sleep.

Then like a birthing head
the lunar circle crowned
between the trees, and lakebed
rocks glowed
luminous as blooms
under black glass.

When she was waterborne, floating
in their midst, they came close
around her bed, to claim
a sister the sky
won't release, but
earth cannot not forget.

BUSH JOURNAL ENTRY #113
Lake Clifton, Yalgorup 2010

At the wetlands
poems grow
from what cannot be collected.

Salt-lake residue
on skin –
ancestral memories.

Heron's lunge or eagle's swoop
that sudden blue
of scattering fairy-wrens.

Wind's insomnia.
Its midday quiet.
Scents of a samphire marsh at sundown.

The full moon on lacustrine thrombolites.
How they build, adapt, sculpt
still life in aragonite.

WAKING UP
at Lake Clifton

Notice the way lake's surface
           moves, wind blown
to where slight waves glint
                     tiny crests
           breaking
on offshore thrombolites
                 blink, blink,
like silver lids
as ripples open
           the wide eye
           of each rock pool
and wink on every stone.

HOMING

Essential in Zen landscapes
white space
separates earth and water.

Blank page or salt-edged lake
it is a place to which
thoughts flock.

UNAWARES IN QUIET

Their arrival catches me unawares in the quiet
between cries, birds that belong here
air-conjured swans flying a line low across the lake.

Behind me a black-faced cuckoo shrike
tries out its song as though for the first
time, as though we've all just come home.

Even the grey teal, sleepy flock
of ducks in a great huddle
at the shoreline, wake
and rise, taking as one to water.

BUSH JOURNAL ENTRY #49

On the lakeside track today, spring showers
then a single shaft of sunlight
breaking through heaven's stained-glass dome
rained down blue shards of splendid fairy-wrens.

SOUNDTRACK

All lake afternoon long
my neighbour the sandplain froglet
sounds like a child
squelching a wet balloon.
It is a lonely game
this hopeful song
he croaks in vain
the same few notes, out
of tune, over
and over again.

FLYING LATE LIGHT

Avocets drift on Lake Clifton
sharp upturned bills feather cushioned
on breasts, at rest red necks
curved. A mild flotilla

though in the air this flock's fluent
geometries of natural order
pattern a wild beauty
deliriously alive

flying late light they wheel and spin
like translucent porcelain, gilt rimmed
their glazes just fired
in the West's blazing kiln.

FOR ONE TREE
elegy for a tuart

Stripped of your crown, your highest branches
bare, sinuous body that once drank light

beggared, now borrows from darkness, stars
for eyes, grows down into the land you rose from.

Learning to let go of drying limbs, you groan.
Earth lends you other voices, singing

long-necked turtles, moist requiems
of sucker-fingered hylid frogs.

Under bark that made bowl and shield
hollows which cradled red-tailed cockatoos

now house feral bees, invading swarms
that fill your empty heart, while lichen

marks your limbs saffron, for burial.

The ringtailed possums cling, as if they knew
we were losing you, Tuart. Where you fork and bend

tangled dodder strings keen in this rising wind
that taps your dead timbers together like clapping sticks.

MANY RIVERS

In the afternoon of life, love at first sight
was always going to be a poem
about loss

a body made of bone and tears, a landscape
of broken shells blown inland from the West,
a shipwreck coast.

This late, love's beginning always follows exile,
its history a long arrival, retold
in a faint accent that has misplaced its country.

Instead, there is a fading memory with a glacier in it
that these lakes invoke, cerulean bloodline
though the ice was not really blue

its heart was a wild and frozen green, forests
buffeted by katabatic winds, egrets
calling above river's running music

all caught in its held breath, in tears
the land would not release for centuries.

They draw me now to country
between wetlands and sea —
sand over limestone, so like the shore

where I left my other skin before
I became estuarine, layered
sweetwater on brine. My ochre heart

bleeds into the ocean. Where it broke
there's a wound that won't heal, once
wrapped in hoar, now sluiced by tides.

Older scars, hardened by salt
winds, read like a map
of the journey from exile

to arrival at these reed-beds
where waves make landfall
and many rivers dream of reaching home.

TREAD KINDLY

When will we tread kindly here
and gentle as ground-water
trickles

between thrombolites
after seeping
through sedge and samphire?

Look, even the trees
spread weightless branches
on this lake,

and lie like perfect
offerings to the clear
light they came from.

THE OLD BRICK KILN

Abandoned, the old kiln
interrupts bushland
with angled redbrick
walls lift oracular holes high,
its four sides enigmatic
in their new life as industrial ruins
lapped by a rising tide of grasses.

Small constellations
of pink fairy orchids
brighten the wasteland,
framed by a disused loading bay.
Inside the furnace mouth, silence
and darkness. Outside, pale stars
shine close to the ground.

NOCTURNE

Where hunted and hungry
go gently into the good night
the deep, diamond
studded dark is not sky.

Nocturnal wetland shrubs
and undergrowth crawl
with nightmares unbound
by dream or sleep.

Don't go barefoot here!
Sac spiders are leaving
their silken retreats, cryptic
prowlers in camouflage

brown stripes, creeping
through reed-shadowed
moonlight to stalk soft–
bodied moths, not

averse to a crusty roach
(unsafe in its carapace when
venom on eight articulated
legs crawls towards dinner)

these predators, armed
with cytotoxin, will bite
your naked toes.

WHITE COCKATOOS

Perched in trees
more leaf than bird
they rise, a winding cloth
        unravelled
        with anguished cries

    reveal dead
    tuart limbs
        jagged as staghorns
        goring the sky.

INTERVAL

If sound is the last sense to leave me
let it be like this evening

under spent storm clouds
seams of sky opened by calm light

loose threads of black swans
flying closer, wings low on the lake.

Coming home from the south
    they pass me with necks outstretched
        like long stitches dusk pulls to the far shore

where they become needlepoint
in the deepening distance above dunes

darning sky's torn hem
invisibly mending the dark.

Let my leaving be like that interval
before stars arrive: a seamless world

all things lost from sight
    only the swans' cries for guidance
        calling a flyway through the night.

WEEPING MYRTLE

They could have been clouds
      those tall oats and wet
      grass where I walked off
      the path, up the rise, leaving

      every name far behind
      me (even my own) until
      I came, innocent of words

      and without map or guide, into
      the shadow of one great tree.

Sitting close I pressed a cheek
      to fissured lifelines, feeling you
      beneath the bark as cool yielding,
      fibrous wood. In my palm

      I warmed a sliver of crushed leaf
      till it released volatile of myrtle.
      Aromatic scents deepened my breath

      breaking me open like a heart, binding me
      to its memories of ancient grief.

When later I wanted to know
     more about the Peppermint
     M. P. told me *that is a women's tree*
     a West Australian with weeping boughs

     healing leaves and ash, stout limb,
     strong wood from which Noongar women

     of this place made digging sticks, wana
     – for protection and for finding food.

HOODED PLOVER

Weeping is permitted in the ruins
of her scrape.

Fragments of unfledged line the sand hollow
where promise died.

A shallow grave for broken shells.

See how they point
to fragile, empty skies.

DESIRE LINES

An Easterly scribbles havoc
flagfall wind-script
in semaphore sedges

winter and dawn
filigree
swamp's fringe

beach spinifex, halophytic
grasses and marram
flex, unquietly.

The regolith is etched
with roo paths and clawprints
bandicootheronrabbitfox.

We focus our telescopes
and settle in
to contemplate shorebirds

among the living rocks –
Woggaal Noorook, fossils
of rare, endangered

DESIRE LINES

communities lost
at ambiguity's edge
on the cusp of living and dying.

Imagine, microbes exhaling
and ozone translating sky
blue, so long ago.

Still breathing water
from out-of-sight aquifers
under the *serpent eggs*

thrombolite
waterstones
old as the Holocene.

Later, we climb eroded ridges
counting how many remnant waders
line the sandbanks to sup on fading light.

I lean against an outcrop, writing
the litany of disappearing names –
hooded plovers, black cockatoos

while behind me on talus slopes of a quarry
wind incenses their absence
in lime-dust.

Air shrouds us
with suspended grit
shape-shifting dunes

surround us with singing sounds
sorrowful as lost lakes
and rising salt.

Sweetwater is eros
in this country, strength
of Peel's supple body

and Yalgorup's wetlands, love
inscribed on earth by time, slowly
discovering her desire lines.

SERPENT SIGN

The dugite is there again today, squeezed
like oil paint from a tube of Vandyke brown
coiled on pale ground where the Bibbulmun track
meets mine. *Serpent: sign of transformation.*

But close up at the crossroads, in the flesh,
polished scales burnt umber and lignite, he
is a muscular god embodied as
pseudo-cobra, lying at my feet curled
asleep in scumbled sand, almost spotlit
by dawn light. I fear its warm incoming
tide will wake him. His head unbends, tongue flicks

sampling the air. Kabarda, spirit king
of a country that tastes me, feels the weight
of this barefoot stranger, sees past her skin.

IN BLOOM

She thought there would be flowers in bloom, fragile sutras
of tissued colour, cupped sepals, calyx, stamen –
she was good at naming the parts.

She thought there would be flowers, wild, yes, not
meadows of delicate translucence, but recondite orchids
offering miniature stained-glass epiphanies.

She did not expect this frayed and salt-sewn backstory
behind the dunes, margin hemmed by hinterland, desolate
as an island between estuary and ocean.

She thought there would be flowers but found instead
a lapidary attraction to landscape's unexpected language
and overlooked songs. She had forgotten how

ubiquitous lamentation and loss, how familiar.
How accomplished she had become
at finding beauty in the barren.

SAMPHIRE AND LIMESTONE

Cupped by sand, three eggs
like lustrous black-speckled pearls
hooded plover's nest
is the tideline's treasure trove,
set in samphire and limestone.

LITANY OF THE WIND

I

Ten lakes, blue water heavy
with memories of sea, bloom
in these salt gardens
hidden between drifting dunes.

Here a patient wind
strings sand like prayer beads
from nightfall to daybreak

threads the singing landscape
through his hands,
reshapes her grain by grain.

2
Indented coves, salt–bitten
scrub, scoured dunes –
litanies of names for periphery.

Sandbar, border,
ecotone and rim
bark, foliage, scales,
meniscus, skin,

plumage, membrane,
tideline, verge,
threshold, littoral,
estuary.

3
Daybreak blurs all words for edge…
kingdoms with no alphabet slip through
sand cordons and the lake bed's skeins
of ravelled light; half-lidded sky broods
above wetlands where a coastal haze is hanging
its threadbare prayer flags on morning's shallow breath.

AT LAST LIGHT

Words arrive
    like sacred ibis
        that fly home at dusk,

           the opening lines
             of evensong
                this lake knows by heart.

WHO, IF

If I should take the wings of morning
Who flies?

If I am never gone from you,
Who dies?

Wind that moves across the waters,
Who breathes?

If losing my life, I find it,
Who leaves?

NO WORD FOR GRIEVING
after Anthony Lawrence

It comes to me unasked
on facebook's news stream
the grace-note of an older word
            —   sillage, *see-yazh* : slipstream
con-trail, wake, tracing things past
by smell or indent; lingering, haptic
imprint of the (still) absent –
airbrushed or watermarked, lent
and transient, what's left when grass is cut.
Gravid with unexpected syllables, my heart
quickens at the stark annunciation
that life goes so fast, a downy-haired girl
who pirouettes beyond view
before the camera clicks
so my photo frames space
remembering her shape, air
shaken as a sprig of wattle
when blue wrens fly away.
And the scent of him, fading
on the green army jumper he wore
when we walked by the lake.
Sillage. I hold it closer. No word for grieving
this, but a whispered presence
like his scarf, still by the door I haven't closed
behind him yet, and loved for that.

THE GUARDIAN TREE

Says it slant, sinuous
pale limbs sky-flung
haloed in winter sun.

Prays with its body,
scrolled paperbark
whispering wind's breviary.

Leans into the light that made it,
lets shade's gentle mercy fall
on salt-bound earth.

Holds fast, old roots
in ageless ground,
guarding lake's threshold.

Grows radiant as a sage
and sometimes, in that voice
Merton heard
        when trees
        said nothing,
speaks to me.

NORTH LAKE DAYBREAK WHEN

chestnut teal ducks stand at rest
along the mudflats,
wearing landscape for plumage,
sunblaze on their breasts.

MY LOVER, THE SEA

Uncovered here, I am a house without
locks, windows wide to skies where nothing holds
      clouds fall apart, light breaks all surfaces.

Discovered here, my porous walls shape rooms
from night's lacustrine dark, take earth's wet scent
for floor and as a roof, the wing-skirr wind
      that talks in peppermints and paperbarks.

Recovered here, my tangled wild glints
in the diamond eyes of webs, dreams
and visions stalk the tree frogs' drum.

My lover the sea arrives salt-skinned and cool
in a mist off the coast, morning comes
like a kiss to the last shore between us.

THE WIND IS AN INSOMNIAC

Spending the dark in scoops
it shadow-sculpts this
slope, these dunes that
wait for first light.

Arriving as it slides
over them like tide,
I am just in time
to photograph sunshine

sluice waves of sand,
wash its pockets
and dimples, brim
in rock pools, those shallow

nests like watergardens
sea creatures weed by day,
where night plants
its stars like seeds.

RENDEZVOUS

Her head lies on damp
sand at the waterline.
Carapace immersed, the long-necked turtle rests
awhile before the arduous climb
up from the lake, counter-
intuitive at any other time

this moving away from the element
that keeps her weightless, moist and safe.

But today she has a rendezvous with life.

Not the full burden of a gravid body
that she drags across dry ground, not
the steep incline nor fear of fox-tailed death
can break the course
that instinct chose for her
from countless generations

that found and climbed this path
before she first drew breath.

And now she has a rendezvous with life

Random, the nature of who lives
or dies. Three or sixteen eggs, her clutch
will not survive unless it's buried deep
on the lakeside of the dune.
At the limits of her strength
she finds a place to labour in, and digs.

Because she has a rendezvous with life.

The formula's precise and imprecise.
Seasonal heat or cold can slow
or speed the incubation that's still weeks
away. And if, once hatched
the neonates delay instead of heading
straight to water, they will

miss their rendezvous with life.

And if the gravid turtle strays beyond
the crest of that first dune, or lays her eggs
in one that's sloping inland, if she stays
off-course, to wander in the bush
for days, drying out and dangerously
exposed to predators, she too will miss

her rendezvous with life.

The double chamber that she's digging
underground must be sound sanctuary
with space for tiny turtles to emerge from
breaking shells. So she conceals the hiding
place, packing the sand hard, slamming it down
with her plastron under-body, heart-beats keeping

the rendezvous with life.

WIND SPEAKS

There's a grief in things
whose names are forgotten
even the wind.

Air, too, is a place
full of contours —
the invisible, mapped
with our breath,
measured in mist
restored by words
remembered.

There's an old language
for this landscape.

It begins with the winds
that made our coastal ridges
crosshatched sands
layered dunes
puckered water
breathed through the reeds.

Surely once there were names
for winds that sift sandhills
shift tidelines of shells
lift flocking birds.

Rainshadow winds, cooling
southwest winds in a season
the Noongar called Djeran, long
before autumn, *mistral, bora, katabatikos* —

This country speaks Binjareb winds,
this ocean's goolamwin – not *foehn,
chinook, barat*, Japan's *oroshi*.
Tell me in Yalgorup's tongue.

There is a grief in things
whose names are forgotten
even the wind.

PETRICHOR

Petrichor, scent of first rainfall on rock,
sedge, sand and trees along this salt-marsh shore
of flooded gums, layers of eucalypt
oil rinsed free releasing its high-pitched tang.

Lower, sultry odours of soaked bark, full
throat-catching cyanobacterial earth smells,
musty geosmin's dark undertones, bank
down the metallic blare of rain-struck stone.

Primal, familiar aromas drone deep
in substrata where soon, lichen and moss
will cast on silent stitches to knit pelts
like coloured maps spread across the wetlands.

Petrichor, nature's soundless mating call
promises new forage. In leaf litter or soil,
seeds and spores stir. Senses, tuned to shifts
of season, lift. Life turns to life and earth
rises like a lover to meet the falling rain.

AFTER DEVOTION

I

The far margin of wintering wetlands,
mist before sunrise. Outside my window
a rock parrot is perched on its fence-post.
All things face east, drawn to the memory
of heat. Except my unassisted heart.

Here, even the lichens have perfected
the art of belonging. Fungal hypha,
appliqued on branch and stone, are hosting
algae. Cells sip the light. Their tattoos map
an ancient coexistence in saffron,
a fluorescent nap on which no X marks
'you are here'. Slow to decode its salt-marsh
lexicon, in this landscape I need more
than time for solitude. I crave belief.

AFTER DEVOTION

2

To you, for the first time (your strength, then,
just rumour, ripeness) my raven lustre
was broken-winged, but not untouchable.

I became your prayer for temptation, you
drank my cup of shame as in acedia,
where the longing for water is holy.

Other men I've known spoke empire, conquest,
riches. You walked on water, considered
the mustard seed, said (beneath a fruitless
tree), 'this cave is a womb of parables'.

Words peeled, leaves curved foetal, pelagic moths
took flight in amniotic sky. *I'd cross*
all lines to talk again if untime could
salve, reprise that other way you spoke.

3

These geckos could be stone. Memory of
breathing reversed. A granite petroglyph,
shade-thin, measures fissures, concavities,
intuits overhangs, angles of descent.

Pre-verbal, instinct risks contact skin first.
As with fingers, mouth, our eyelids opaque,
we sensed flesh as lizards might feel country,
spines to sun. Reading its touch, we lay soft-
bellied, uncut on obsidian blades.

I trusted contours until your spittle
and clay healed my eyes, opened me to day's
brittle light, its delible vows. *Translate
me from doubt*, I prayed, knowing all mirage
was lie, wanting to believe your version.

4

Will you return? Once, before autumn dusk
swallowed stump and roo, I saw a shadow,
thought I heard the almost music of you.
Was that just the lake, little rock pools lipped
by breakgrace ripples, reed-hushed, reaching shore?

The last hour of light is holiest,
water and incense, litanies of frog
choirs in stalls of sideways sun; midges,
dust motes spiralling the treeline to smoke.

I was your devotee. You were moisture
soaking beneath salt-crusts. You were landfall
to exhausted flocks. Your presence promised
seasons of seepage after drought. When you
breathed, rainclouds formed like pietà on the hills.

5

No more. The wedgetail's sharp diagonal
is etched on clear evening sky. Beneath him,
high in the acacia, a lizard slows
as daylight ebbs, muscles grow cold. Expect
a death. Over wild landscape – north east south
west – the raptor wheels. I watch, want to catch
his dive, wait (as I always wait) for night

to unlatch its mouth. After devotion,
this is left: writing on air; vigilant
silence (dark's relation, its other self);
litanies of lost names, hooded plover,
black cockatoo. I have kept only your
bright aleph, first letter which divided
all horizons and may still bring down walls.

6

On this night, Arctic's curlew sandpipers
arrive like *petit point* crossing the moon,
descend with aching wings and hearts that thread
the hessian salt-marsh to pellucid sky.

They shed flight's wind-worn robe, its ravelled seams,
creases which charted paths to sanctuaries
like these, where ghostly frames retrieve their strength.
I recognise their exiles' weariness.

We are all wayfinders at journey's end,
reprieved by patchwork wetlands, these furthest
outposts of spring. Seasons have passed. *I changed
my life* and at first light, will watch them wade,
curved bills stitching water, insistently dip
dipping, feeding the hunger to leave.

TRACINGS

Sometimes we misplace
the map of who we are.

Walking Yalgorup
that first time

on crumpled limestone,
by brittle lakebeds

past wiry reeds, under
shedding paperbarks,

I remembered.

NOTES TO THE POEMS

'The practice of belonging' is set in Denmark, on Australia's SW coast, where I had intended settling, before Yalgorup. Its italicised phrases are from my previously published poems 'The Clearing' and 'Curled', published in *The Roof Milkers*, Sunline, 2008; and 'Paper, Ink, Inkstone, Brushes', which won the Creatrix Prize in 2008, and was first published in *Indigo*, vol. 3, 2009. This poem has also been published in *Dark Diamonds*, an anthology by Mt Hallowell Press in 2012, and in *Poetry d'Amour* by WA Poets Inc. in 2013.

   The boobook (*Ninox novaeseelandiae ocellata*) and kookaburra (*Dacelo novaeguineae*), or laughing kookaburra; the latter is a large Australian kingfisher, not native to WA, but which became ubiquitous in the South West following its release from Perth Zoo in the early twentieth century; both birds are now almost as iconic as the blue wrens in Denmark.

'Heron on the rocks' was first published in *Creatrix* no. 9, Perth, 2010; recorded on Bush Journal CD limited edition 2011. The zen imagery was suggested by Andrew Lansdown's poem *Warrior Monk* and my own observations of *Egretta novaehollandiae* wading among thrombolites at Lake Clifton, Yalgorup National Park.

'Woggaal Noorook' (formerly 'Breath') – the image of windows was suggested by the following mention of fenestrae: 'The fenestrae within the thrombolites provide habitats for isopods, amphipods, coleopteran and thichopteran larvae, shrimps and juvenile gobiid fishes', in an email (9 September 2009) from Laurie Smith. His source is the mid-conference excursion guidebook from the International Symposium on Foraminifera, Perth, 2002. By association, breath and lungs in this poem allude to the oxygenation of our planet by these earliest life forms, the photosynthesising bacteria which live in symbiotic relationship with the thrombolites they 'build'.

   This poem was chosen as the 2012 Stretch Festival of Art and Culture theme and the performance script for the 2010 Stretch Festival: dance/music/poetry opening performance at Mandurah Performing Arts Centre Directed by Helen Duncan, Choreography by Helen Duncan and Lee West, Musicians George Walley (didgeridoo) and Tristen Parr (cello); Poetry by Annamaria Weldon, Dancers Laura Boynes, Helen Duncan and Lee West.

'The memory of earth' was first published in *Westerly* vol. 56, no. 1, 2011. This poem references the Pinjarra Massacre of 1834, where a party of men, led by Governor James Stirling, surrounded the camp of the Bindjareb Noongars in Pinjarra and opened fire. Bindjareb Noongar cultural teacher George Walley showed me this place, told me its history, named the dwellings mia mias, the season Kambarang and

238

the Murray River Bilya Maadjit in his traditional language. In writing this poem I was also deeply influenced by artworks in the Pinjarra Massacre Memorial Exhibition. 'The memory of earth' was awarded The 2010 Tom Collins Poetry Prize by the Fellowship of Australian Writers WA. The quote at the top of this poem is taken from the appeal for a memorial, viewed on www.pinjarramassacresite.com.

'Birthbed' is set in Yalgorup National Park, at the viewing platform at Lake Clifton's thrombolite reef. On 7 January 2010, the *Thrombolite (microbialite) Community of a Coastal Brackish Lake (Lake Clifton)* was listed as critically endangered under the *Environment Protection and Biodiversity Conservation Act 1999* (EPBC Act).

'Bush journal entry #113' was first published as part of the image-text exhibition *What cannot be collected* by Perdita Phillips in 2010. Aragonite is a crystalline form of calcium carbonate produced by the mainly filamentous cyanobacteria *Scytonema*, a process which results in structures now known as thrombolites, a term first introduced by the late Dr Linda Moore during her extensive research at Lake Clifton.

Bush journal entry #49 was first published in *Indigo*, vol. 5, Summer 2010; recorded on *Bush Journal* installation CD; and featured as part of the text and image installation of the same name, created in collaboration with artist Carolyn Marks for the opening of INQB8 Centre for Contemporary Art in Mandurah, WA.

'Flying late light' was first published in *Westerly*, vol. 55, no. 2, 2010.

'For one tree' was recorded for Jukebox CD in *dotdotdash* no. 06, Perth, 2011. The tuart, *Eucalyptus gomphocephala*, has been undergoing an alarming period of decline in the Yalgorup region of south-western Australia. This tree plays a vital role for many living creatures of its ecosystem. 'The number of scarred tuart trees in the forest indicate usage by Aboriginal people. The trunks were cut and the bark removed for shields and utensils' (George Walley personal communication, 2009).

Dodder laurel is a parasitic, tree-climbing vine with a tangled growth habit. Ring-tailed possum *Pseudocheirus occidentalis* now nationally listed as vulnerable, is endemic to Yalgorup National Park. A marsupial, it is an arboreal feeder most at home in the trees.

Singing long-necked turtles, also known as oblong turtles, alludes to research by Dr Jaqueline Giles, who identified the complex acoustic repertoire used by *Chelodina oblonga* turtles to communicate underwater.

Hylid frogs: the slender tree-frog – *Litoria adelaidensis* – and the Western green tree-frog – *Litoria moorei*.

'Many rivers' was first published in *dotdotdash*, no. 4, Autumn 2010. 'Many rivers' references the waterways and wetlands of the Peel–Harvey region, but takes poetic licence in its allusion to a glacier; for while the coastal lakes of Yalgorup were formed following the last great ice-melt that altered global ocean levels, the southern continent of Australia was not itself subject to glaciation in such recent times.

'The old brick kiln' was first published online in *Landscape*, Edith Cowan University 2010. Between 1922 and 1923, a rotary kiln was constructed to burn the shells to lime at Lake Clifton. It operated for just two weeks and was then closed as it did not work successfully. The rotary kiln itself has been removed but the brick structure that was used to support it is in very good condition. Source: Lake Clifton Herron Progress and Sporting Association Inc., 2012.

NOTES TO THE POEMS

'**Nocturne**' was first published in *dotdotdash*, vol. 4, 2010. The giant sac spider – *Miturga agelenina* – prowls at night and has a nasty cytotoxic bite. I became interested after finding and photographing an intricately crafted 'retreat': the sac spider weaves a beautiful, complex pouch of silken threads as its daytime resting place.

'**Interval**' featured as the final panel of Carolyn Marks' *Bush Journal*, a charcoal and sculpture installation at INQB8 Centre for Contemporary Art, Mandurah, based on eleven of my poems which I recorded for the soundtrack, and which were included as text as part of the visual images. On the opening night of the *Stretch Festival 2010*, at the Mandurah Performing Arts Centre, I read this poem to live didgeridoo and cello music, during a contemporary dance sequence which was choreographed around five of my Lake Clifton poems, and staged to a backdrop of my nature photos. In 2012 it formed part of a longer ensemble piece which again launched the festival.

'**Hooded plover**' – *Thinornis rubricollis* is endemic to Australia, but listed as near threatened in WA; Yalgorup is a significant breeding wetland for them. Their eggs, laid in a shallow sand-scrape on exposed beaches, are often taken by predators (foxes, gulls) or crushed by careless humans walking dogs, or riding horses or quad bikes. Sources: BirdLife Australia and Dr Grainne Maguire, on-site workshop, Lake Pollard Yalgorup National Park 2012, which I attended. The first words echo Ian Burgham's opening line 'Longing is permitted amongst the ghost voices' from his poem 'What's to become of us', *The Stone Skippers*, Maclean Dubois, Edinburgh, 2007.

'**Desire lines**' was first published in *The Disappearing*, an online App by The Red Room Company, 2012. Woggaal Noorook is the Noongar Bindjareb term for the thrombolites at Lake Clifton, which translates as 'eggs of the creation serpent'.

'**Serpent sign**' – my memorable encounter with a dugite *Pseudonaja affinis*, the most common dangerously venomous snake in the Perth region, is behind this poem. Its Noongar name is *kabarda*. The Bibbulmun Track stretches nearly 1000 km from the hills on the outskirts of Perth, to Albany on the south coast. Reserved for walkers, its yellow triangular markers symbolise the 'Woggaal' – the rainbow serpent of the Aboriginal Dreaming.

'**In bloom**' – 'a lapidary attraction to landscape's unexpected language' is a reference to the stone reef landscape at Lake Clifton and limestone outcrops in this national park. *Sutra* is a Sanskrit word meaning 'binding thread'. 'In Bloom' was first published online by Australian Poetry as poem of the week in 2012.

240

'**No word for grieving**', after Anthony Lawrence's 'A Sound For Leaving', *Signal Flare*, Puncher & Wattman, Glebe, 2013.

'**The guardian tree**' – saltwater paperbark *Melaleuca cuticularis*. The last stanza is a reference to *When the trees say nothing*, (Thomas Merton 1915–68) edited by Kathleen Deignan with a foreword by Thomas Berry, published by Sorin Books, Notre Dame, Indiana, 2003. With acknowledgment to Emily Dickinson's line' Tell all the Truth but tell it slant', Poem 1129, *The Complete Poems*.

'**My lover, the sea**' – former UK poet laureate Andrew Motion is lobbying for the retention of the word 'skirr', a whirring or grating sound made by wings of birds in flight. See <http://www.telegraph.co.uk/news/uknews/3046488/Collins-dictionary-asks-public-to-rescue-outdated-words.html>.

'**Wind speaks**' – Yalgorup is a coastal wetlands and national park on the south-west coast of Western Australia. The traditional language is Bindjareb, a Noongar dialect particular to the Pinjarra area. 'Wind Speaks' was first published online in *Landscape*, ECU 2010; recorded for *Bush Journal* installation and CD for INQB8 Centre for Contemporary Art, Mandurah, WA; performed at Stretch Festival launch at the Mandurah Performing Arts Centre 2010 and 2012.

'**Petrichor**' was published in the anthology *Science Made Marvellous*, Poets Union Inc., Potts Point, NSW, 2010 for National Science Week 2010. Petrichor is that specific scent of rain on dry ground and is caused by the sluicing of water to dissolve oils exuded by certain plants during hot weather, together with the compound *geosmin*, which is produced by several classes of microbes, including cyanobacteria, which has an earthy smell. The term, from the Greek for rock – *petra* – and the Greek mythological word for fluid that flows in the veins of the Gods – *ichor* – was coined by two Australian researchers, Bear and Thomas, for an article in Nature.

'**After devotion**' was first published in *Australian Book Review* no. 339, 2012. In this version of the poem, the final line of the first sonnet has been altered from the original published in the ABR when it was shortlisted for the Peter Porter Poetry Prize: 'I crave [want – *original*] belief'.
      This poem's many references include: Sonnet 1: 'My unassisted heart is barren clay / Which of its native self can nothing feed:', *To The Supreme Being*, a poem by Michelangelo Buonarroti (1475–1564). This poem was translated into English by William Wordsworth (1770–1850), <http://www.poetry-archive.com/b/to_the_supreme_being. html>; Barbara York Main's writing on lichen, hypha and algae in *Between Wodjil and Tor*, Landfall Press, Perth, 1967; Sonnet 2: Acedia, a spiritual affliction the Desert Fathers called 'dryness of the soul', from Kathleen Norris' *Amazing Grace*, Penguin, New York, 1999; Sonnet 4: breakgrace: 'from the lines of breakgrace / in a leaf, a face', *Abyss of Light*, sonnets by the US poet T. Zachary Cotler (unpublished); Pietà as in the name and shape of Michelangelo's famous Carrara marble statue; Sonnet 5: Lizards' energy wanes at sunset so they are often caught by raptors such as the wedgetail eagle *Aquila audax* if they become stranded in high branches, from personal communication with naturalist Laurie Smith; A Sufi story, 'the Aleph which brought down a wall', retold by Vivienne Robertson at the Conference on Nature, Religion and Culture, UWA, Perth WA, December 2010; Sonnet 6: The curlew sandpiper *Calidris ferruginea* flies annually from Siberia to the Yalgorup, a RAMSAR-listed protected wetlands on Western Australia's coast. 'I have changed my life' responds to Rainer Maria Rilke's poem 'Archaic Torso of Apollo' in *Ahead of All Parting. Selected poetry and prose of Rainer Maria Rilke*, Trans. Stephen Mitchell, Modern Library, New York, 1995.

ACKNOWLEDGMENTS

In sharing their sense of place with me, many people made this book a possibility. I'm grateful for their conversations, fieldtrips, workshops, symposia, research, loan of treasured texts and lifetimes of commitment to country. And though I've named several here, *The Lake's Apprentice* also owes a debt to the diverse communities of Mandurah, which is truly a 'meeting place of the heart', for years of friendship, hospitality and assistance. I make no claim to expert or exhaustive coverage in this book, however, and any misrepresentations or mistakes in it are my own. This is a personal impression of the Yalgorup National Park, wetlands and thrombolites; the photos I took on my Kodak Z8612IS, the books I read are generally available and I've listed them for other persistent wanderers to find.

The catalyst to this book was a writing residency at SymbioticA UWA where, in collaboration with Laurie Smith, an erudite naturalist and raconteur, for eighteen months I researched and developed the *Adaptation* eco-art project 'Sharing the Edge'. Our director Oron Catts encouraged creative freedom within a network of scientists- and artists-in-residence from around the world. They included Australia's Carmel Wallace, Perdita Phillips, Catherine Higham and Vyonne Walker, who with Art Curator Amanda Alderson (then our project manager) have continued to influence and encourage me. Thank you all!

However, I would not have written about the wetlands in quite the same way without the friendship of George Walley, Bindjareb Noongar cultural leader and music man, and the guidance of Gloria Kearing, Bindjareb Noongar elder, artist and educator. They welcomed me to country and showed me something of the traditional Bindjareb relationship to place. Equally welcoming and indispensable were environmentalist Nancy Fardin and her artist husband Galliano; they read and informed my writing, often nourishing me with good food and stories at their lake-shore home. The artist, Mandurah gallery curator and former Stretch Festival Art Director, Carolyn Marks has been a dream collaborator down the years, intuitively developing visual forms to go with my words on the page, screen, stage and installation, including *Bush Journal* 2012, from which we have taken her flocking birds for the pages of Nature Notes and the poems. Peel-Harvey Catchment Council's Jane O'Malley and Christine Comer involved me in their conservation projects, and Jane Tillson, Lee Kennedy, Rebecca Nelson and Barb Thomas created many opportunities for me to engage with their community as a visiting writer, supporting my research and development with their artistic and logistical skills. I am grateful beyond telling for their kindness and knowledge. The enthusiasm of former mayor Paddy Creevy, local member for Mandurah David Templeman, Chair of the Peel–Harvey Catchment Council Jan Star, and John Hughes from the City of Mandurah for my involvement in their community life has also been pivotal.

Dick Rule (BirdLife Australia), Brett Brenchley (Coordinator Climate Change Services at the City of Mandurah), Dr Jacqueline Giles (Wetland Ecologist), Dr Katinka Ruthrof (State Centre of Excellence for Climate Change, Woodland and Forest Health Biological Sciences and Biotechnology Murdoch University), Dr John C. Ryan (post-doctoral research fellow at Edith Cowan University), Dr Glen Phillips (Director, International Centre for Landscape and Language at Edith Cowan University), Dr Glenn Albrecht (Professor of Sustainability, and Director, Institute for Sustainability and Technology Policy, Murdoch University) all deserve special mention for so generously sharing their expertise whenever consulted in a spirit of friendship, greatly helping my unfunded and independent explorations. As did Alex Chapman (research scientist, W.A. Herbarium), encountered in the manuscript's last stages, but by no means least in his contribution.

I also want to acknowledge the pioneering geobiological research of Dr Linda Moore (1956–2010), and that of Professor Neville Stanley who invited Linda to become his doctoral research student in the Department of Microbiology at the University of Western Australia. I was given the background to this by Dr Robert Burne, visiting fellow at the Research School of Earth Sciences at Australian National University, whose subsequent research collaboration with Dr L. Moore led to a publication (Burne & Moore 1987) in which a new overall term 'microbialite' was coined, in reference to the Lake Clifton thrombolites.

For their perceptive readings and responses to some of the poems and essays in The Lake's Apprentice, I thank Rachel Robertson, Mark Tredinnick, Peter Bishop and Amanda Curtin. I am also grateful to Roland Leach, Dennis Haskell, Horst Kornberger and Trisha Kotai-Ewers (Fellowship of Australian Writers WA); Peter Rose (Australian Book Review); Donna Ward (Indigo and Inkerman & Blunt); Paula and Rob McLean (The Nature Conservancy Australia) and Lucy Dougan (Westerly) for their persistent belief in my writing.

I am delighted that Nicolas Rothwell and Barry Lopez agreed to read The Lake's Apprentice, and kindly gave permission to publish their comments.

Despite my frequent disappearances due to wetland wanderings or writing, my friends Rose van Son, Jo Clarke, Tineke Van der Ecken, Viv Glance, Mags Webster, Caroline Crichton, Liana Joy Christensen, Bernadette Aitken, Amanda Joy, Nandi Chinna and the 'Out of the Asylum Writers' have been constant companions whose kindness and belief in this book was crucial, and I thank them for it!

My son Roger Castillo and my daughter Veronica Morgan have sustained me with their love, and patiently shared me all of their lives with 'the writing', so it is a joy to dedicate this book to them. And, for the opportunity to do so, I am extremely grateful to UWA Publishing, in particular visionary Director Terri-ann White and editor Anne Ryden, who relished every challenge, turned the publishing process into a joy for me and saw from the start what kind of book my manuscript could become.

LIST OF PHOTOS

Photography by Annamaria Weldon

246

FURTHER READING

I am an avid reader and without these books my understanding of place would be poorer. This list is followed by a list of the books I consulted to compile the scientific names, together with *FloraBase – the Western Australian Flora* which is the authoritative online information system on WA's indigenous and naturalised plants.

Carter, Bevan and Lynda Nutter, *Nyungah Land: records of invasion and theft of Aboriginal land on the Swan River 1829–1850*, Black History Series, Swan Valley Nyungah Community, Guildford, 2005.

Cathcart, Michael, *The Water Dreamers*, Text, Melbourne, 2009.

Davis, Wade, *The Wayfinders. Why ancient wisdom matters in a modern world*, UWA Publishing, Crawley, 2009.

Deakin, Roger, *Notes from Walnut Tree Farm*, Penguin, Sydney, 2008.

Giblett, Rod and Hugh Webb (eds), *Western Australian Wetlands: the Kimberley and South West*, Black Swan Press & Wetlands Conservation Society (inc.), 1996.

Gray, Robert, *The Land I Came Through Last*, Giramondo, Artarmon, 2008.

Hill, Barry and John Wolseley, *Lines for Birds*, UWA Publishing, Crawley, 2011.

Hughes, Ted, *Poetry in the Making*, Faber & Faber, London, 1967.

Lopez, Barry and Debra Gwartney, *Home Ground Language for an American Landscape*, Trinity University Press, San Antonio, 2006.

Mabey, Richard, *A Brush with Nature: 25 years of personal reflections on nature*, BBC Books, Random House NZ, 2010.

Nikulinsky, Phillippa and Stephen D. Hopper, *Life on the Rocks*, Fremantle Press, Fremantle, 2008.

Rothwell, Nicolas, *Journeys to the Interior*, Black Inc, Collingwood, 2010.

Sacks, Oliver, 'Oaxaca Journal', *National Geographic*, 2002.

Seddon, George, *Sense of Place*, UWA Press, Nedlands, 1972.

Tredinnick, Mark (ed), *A Place on Earth: an anthology of nature writing from Australia and North America*, University of Nebraska Press, Lincoln, 2003.

Tredinnick, Mark, *The Land's Wild Music*, Trinity University Press, San Antonio, 2005.

Vanclay, Frank, Mathew Higgins, Adam Blackshaw (eds), *Making Sense of Place*, National Museum of Australia, Canberra, 2009.

York Main, Barbara, *Between Wodjil and Tor*, Jacaranda Press, Landfall Press, Brisbane, 1967.

Books consulted in compiling a list of scientific names for *The Lake's Apprentice*:

Brown, Andrew, Pat Dundas, Kingsley Dixon and Stephen Hopper, *Orchids of Western Australia*, UWA Press, Crawley, 2008.

Lane, Peter *Geology of Western Australia's National Parks: geology for everyone*, Peter Lane, Margaret River, 2004 and 2007 (2nd edn).

McNamara, Ken, *Stromatolites*, Western Australian Museum, Perth, 2009.

Neville, Simon, *Travellers Guide to the Parks and Reserves of Western Australia*, Fremantle, 2006 (3rd edn).

Neville, Simon and Nathan McQuoid, *Guide to the Wildflowers of South Western Australia*, Fremantle, 1998.

Orange, Paul, David Knowles, Gilbert White, Gerhardt Sauracker and Simon Neville, *Guide to the Wildlife of the Perth Region*, Simon Neville Publications, Perth, 2005.

Ramage, Jan with illustrations by Ellen Hickman, *Tuart Dwellers*, Department of Environment and Conservation, Western Australia, 2008/9.

Rippey, Elizabeth and Barbara Rowland, *Coastal Plants Perth and the South West Region*, UWA Press, Nedlands WA 1995 and 2004 (2nd edn).

Ryan, John Charles, *Green Sense: the aesthetics of plants, place and language*, Truehart Academic, Oxford, 2012.

Scott, Jane and Patricia Negus, *Field Guide to the Wildflowers of Australia's South West*, Cape to Cape Publishing, North Fremantle, 2002.

Smith, G. G., *A Guide to the Coastal Flora of South-Western* Australia Handbook No. 10, Western Australian Naturalists Club, Perth, 1973.